Children Of The Holocaust
Tell Their Stories

Children Of The Holocaust
Tell Their Stories

Edited by Wendy Whitworth

Quill

in association with

THE
HOLOCAUST
CENTRE

Journeys

Children Of The Holocaust Tell Their Stories

Edited by Wendy Whitworth

Published in Great Britain by
Quill Press in association with The Holocaust Centre
The Hub,
Haskell House,
152 West End Lane
London.
NW6 1SD

British Library Catalogue in Publication Data
A catalogue record for this book is available from the
British Library.

ISBN 0-9555009-4-X
978-0-9555009-4-7

Design and artwork: The Holocaust Centre
Printed and bound by MPG Biddles Ltd

*To all the children
whose stories were never told*

CONTENTS

CONTENTS

Introduction

Just imagine for a moment that you are ten years old and something really significant happens in your life. Maybe a relative dies or your parents split up; maybe you have a new brother or sister; or you move to a different country with new friends and a new language to learn. When those big things happen in our lives, we often remember them quite vividly. Many years later, they still stand out and we can talk about them. I remember that my parents were thinking about leaving their jobs and setting up a new house when I was ten. Even now, I remember the discussions and the uncertainty – and the move we made a few months later.

Then imagine being a child and having your whole world turned upside down. Imagine being separated from your parents, being made to hide, or losing your brothers and sisters. Imagine being sent to another country, or to a family you do not know, or being moved into a tiny space with very little food and water, or not being able to go out to play in case you were caught. If you had lived through times when you feared for your life every day and wondered why the world was always a place of sadness, then the memories would stand out very clearly.

In this book, you will find 30 short stories of children who had some of those very painful memories. They were all born shortly before the Second World War and lived as Jewish children during the time of Adolf Hitler and the Nazis. Because they were Jewish, their lives were at risk. Some of the children in this book were lucky and were sent to safety in England before the war. Others were not so lucky and were left behind in countries where the Nazis were killing Jewish people.

All of the people whose stories are included in this book have one thing in common – they were saved by grown-ups who did everything they could to look after them. It did not mean they had happy stories, but at least they managed to survive and start their lives again after the end of the war.

They have all told their very long stories in just six pages, so that you can read them easily and hear one or two things they have learned from their experiences. Some of them have also written a whole book just about their own life story, so you can imagine how difficult it was to make it short enough to fit into six pages. But at least this way, you can read about a lot of people and see just how different their life stories are.

The book is called *Journeys* because all the people in it have helped create an exhibition at the Holocaust Centre in England, called *The Journey*. In that museum, they have made a video about their life, or they go there regularly to meet the visitors and talk to young people about their life story.

These 30 people are not children any more. Most of them have their own grandchildren and they are nearly all over 70 years old. But they remember very clearly what happened to them when they were very young. They tell the story of their journey at that time because they want us to know what happened. They also hope that we will learn something about the way people behave towards each other, because they want the world to be a better place for the children of today.

You will not enjoy all these stories because many are quite sad. But, hopefully, you will find the journeys interesting, with something you can think about, talk about, and learn from, too.

Stephen D. Smith
Executive Director, Shoah Foundation Institute,
Los Angeles
July 2009

Acknowledgements

My warmest thanks and admiration go first and foremost to the survivors who have cooperated so effectively in the creation of this volume. Working with them to adapt their stories for primary-age readers has been an unforgettable and humbling experience for me, and I have learned so much from their example of courage and resilience. I thank them sincerely for the use of their stories and personal photographs.

I would also like to thank *The Journey* exhibition team at the Holocaust Centre, and in particular Vanessa Hopkinson, Head of Primary Education, Karen Van Coevorden, Primary Education and Training Officer, and Aneesa Riffat, Museum and Education Officer. Their collaboration has been invaluable in ensuring that the stories are appropriate for the 10-11 age group. Sincerest thanks also go to Glen Powell, the Holocaust

Centre's designer, who has created a most attractive book which we hope will entice younger readers.

Perhaps most important of all, this book could never have been published without the remarkable vision and unfailing support of the Smith family – Marina, Eddie, Stephen and James – whose work in the field of Holocaust education and genocide prevention is inspiring and second to none.

Wendy Whitworth
July 2009

Ruth, aged three, in Berlin

Ruth Barnett

"Are we nearly there yet?"

My name is Ruth Barnett and I was born in Berlin in January 1935. My father was a young lawyer and his mother had a cinema advertising business, so our family was quite well off. My mother was a secretary and when they married, she helped run the family business. My brother, Martin, was three years older than me and we used to play together a lot. We were just an ordinary German family until I was four years old.

But when Hitler came to power in Germany, things changed and Jews were in danger. My father was Jewish and managed to escape just in time to Shanghai in China, one of the few countries Jews could go to. My mother wasn't Jewish and was therefore relatively safe. But one day she took part in a protest march when the Nazis said that German people married to Jews had to divorce them. All the protesters were arrested. My mother never talked to me about what happened to them, but she was in hiding in Germany during the war.

My parents were obviously worried about what might happen to Martin and me. They took the very difficult decision to send us away on the *Kindertransport*, (Children's transport) to England. I had no idea this was going to happen. Martin says that he was prepared and given English lessons in advance, but I wasn't.

I remember going in a car, presumably a taxi, and it was just like going on an outing somewhere. I remember being excited. We went to the station and I threw a tantrum because we were near Berlin zoo and I wanted to go there and not to England. That left me feeling that I was a bad girl because I'd made a fuss. I got it into my head that I'd been sent away from Germany because I was bad.

I can remember the train journey because it took forever and I got fed up. I kept saying, "Are we nearly there yet?" The next thing I remember, I was being woken from a deep sleep because we'd reached the coast. Then I remember getting onto the boat. It seemed absolutely enormous to me and I got very anxious because hundreds of people were pouring on. I started to worry about how the boat could possibly float with all those people on it. But my brother reassured me – and that set a pattern right through our time in England without our parents. Whatever my brother said made things OK. He really became like my mother. Our parents' last words to him were, "Look after your little sister."

My mother travelled with us on the train to England. She was able to get a holiday visa because she wasn't Jewish and she took us to our first foster family. Then she had to go back. The strange thing is that neither Martin nor I remember saying goodbye to her. I imagine it was too painful for us.

Our first foster father was an elderly clergyman in Kent and I remember him with great affection. He used to take us for walks and taught me to love the countryside. But his wife was many years younger and I don't think she wanted to look after somebody else's children. She didn't have any children of her own and she was cruel to us. I won't say we were unhappy. We were struggling to survive because we didn't know anything else. We stayed with them altogether for four years.

I remember being desperate to please and be a good girl so I would be allowed to go back to my parents. But I was always getting everything wrong. I couldn't understand the English words, but I knew I was being scolded. I knew I was a bad girl, particularly when I wet the bed and my foster mother beat me with a leather strap.

That nightmare went on for two years until we went to a Quaker boarding school. After that, we just went back to Kent for holidays. The school matron took me into the dormitory and showed me how every bed had a rubber sheet on it. She said, "Everybody wets the bed when they first come here." And I don't remember having a problem after that.

After two years at school, we went to a hostel for homeless children in Richmond, London. It was chaotic because by then it was the middle of the war, but we stayed there one summer. After that, we went to a second foster family in Kent, who had five children of their own. I was very happy there, especially because their daughter, Joan, was exactly the same age as me. We kept in touch permanently afterwards.

But then we had to move to a third foster family who were farmers. I didn't understand why we had to move. I thought the second family had got fed up with me because I was too naughty. Actually, it was because my brother was very disturbed by the doodlebugs or flying bombs that came over our house.

I was about nine years old when I became aware that I was Jewish. The other kids in the playground had somehow figured out that I was from Germany – even though I had no accent at all. They started calling me a Nazi and doing the Hitler salute. I insisted that I couldn't be a Nazi because I wasn't even German and I'd been kicked out of Germany because I was a Jew. That's when I developed my Jewish identity.

For ten years, Martin and I somehow managed to survive like this. We had no contact with our mother at all. I don't know whether she wrote any letters. I remember our father visited us in England on his way to Shanghai. He got a boat from Southampton and took my brother to London for a few days. It was terrifying for me because I thought my brother had abandoned me. After that, he promised he'd never leave me again, and I don't think he did, not until I was old enough to understand. For those ten years, I told myself that my mother was dead. I remember people asking me, "Where is your mother?" and I simply said she was dead.

That made it very difficult for me when my mother came to England after the war and wanted to take me back to Germany. By then I was 14. I had a picture in my mind of this terrible place called Germany where people did terrible things, so the idea of going there was impossible. And I couldn't grasp that this total stranger was my mother. She didn't look like anything I could remember. She didn't speak a word of English and I didn't speak a word of German. I remember feeling totally confused. I just didn't want my life disturbed again.

My third foster family said I could stay with them and my mother went back alone. I felt quite awful about rejecting her, but I couldn't deal with it at the time. Then later, my foster mother took me back to

Germany and left me there. That was a terrible time for me and I found it hard to make a new relationship with my parents.

My brother stayed in England and went to Cambridge University, where he met a lovely German girl. They got married later and he willingly settled in Germany and still lives there. We're still very close and I go and visit him two or three times a year.

Of course, these experiences profoundly affected me, but I'm very satisfied with what I've been able to make of my life. I have a wonderful husband, three lovely children and two lovely grandchildren. I worked as a teacher for 19 years and I think I've contributed to education. I decided to talk in schools about my experiences. This is very important to me because I feel that education is the way forward for humanity. We need to know about the horrible things in the past so that we have a bit more control over the spread of violence in the future. Although we look different and our body shape, skin and hair colour may be different, we are all human beings. I would like young people to think a lot more about how similar we all are.

"Are we nearly there yet?"

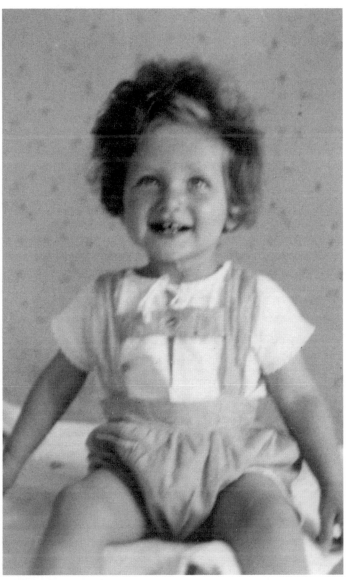

Ruth, aged two, in Berlin

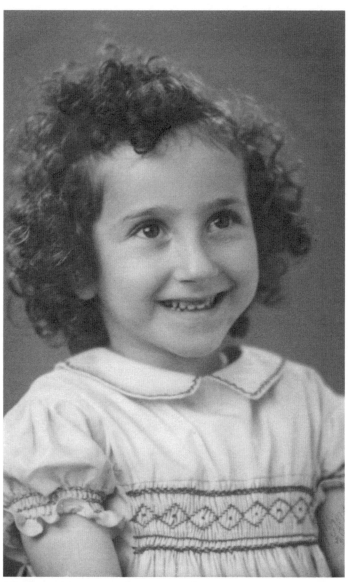

Blanche, aged four, in Copenhagen, Denmark

BLANCHE BENEDICK

The courage of Danish people

My name is Blanche Benedick and I was born in Copenhagen, Denmark, on 20 September 1933. My father had a small factory. He was a wonderful man who could turn his hand to anything to look after the family. My mother always seemed to be in the kitchen. I remember coming home from school and being greeted by delicious cooking smells. I had an older brother and sister from my father's first marriage and my younger sister was born later, in Sweden.

We lived in a second-floor flat in a mainly Jewish area in Copenhagen. It was a traditional Jewish home and we lit our candles every Friday night. We didn't go to synagogue every Saturday, but we always went at festival times. Before the war, we also kept the special dietary rules at home.

I have very clear memories of the festival of Passover. Grandfather would go through all the prayers and songs from beginning to end – which takes hours! I was only about 10 and we weren't allowed to eat until he had finished – about 11p.m! I used to sit and look at the painting on the wall – a table with a big bunch of grapes – and I used to count the grapes. I still have that painting at home today and I treasure it.

As a child, I liked sports and singing, but I also loved playing outdoors. I had my dolls and pram and used to take them for walks on Sundays with Mona, my friend from across the road.

Mona was my best friend, but she wasn't Jewish. We went to school on the same tram, although to different schools. I started at a Jewish school when I was about seven and can remember my first day. We had to wear little aprons and the first class was like nursery school; you learnt a few things and got used to playing with other children. I stayed at that school until I was ten.

When war broke out and the Germans invaded Denmark in 1940, we suffered the same curfews and rationing as other countries, and there was bombing. We had to run down to the cellar whenever there were air raids. There was a lot of talk about the Jewish people – that things were going to get worse for them.

One day at school, the headmaster called me into his office and said, "You know there's a war on?" And I replied, "Of course I do." By then I was ten and knew what was happening. He went on, "Well, Mona's mother came to see me today and said you have to go back to their house this afternoon. Your mother and father are there as well." So I went back to Mona's after school.

My mother was sitting crying and my father was pacing up and down, looking worried. Mona's mother said, "Don't worry, Blanche, you're going to stay here with us for a few days. We're going to hide you because we've heard that all the Jews are going to be rounded up. That was in October 1943.

Like many ordinary Danish people, Mona's parents were wonderful and did so much to help us – even though they were risking their own lives. There were about 8,000 Jewish people in Copenhagen at the time – and only 450 were caught. Mona's father was a keen photographer and had a dark room to develop his pictures. He told me, "If you hear the Nazi police coming up the stairs, run into that little room and keep very quiet." The police actually came twice and it was very scary!

We stayed there for about four days, but it wasn't safe for Mona's parents to keep us very long. They arranged a taxi to take us to the coast – because our aim was to go by boat across to Sweden, which wasn't involved in the war. I remember that in the taxi, my father gave me some money and said, "Keep that safe in your pocket. We're going to hide you under the rug, so if we get stopped, they might not see you. If we're separated, you've got your whole life ahead of you and might have a chance of being saved." Fortunately, we were not stopped.

At the coast, we went to a big hut where the fishermen kept the catch of the day. There were some other Jewish people waiting there, but because my mother was pregnant, the fishermen took us in the first boat. There were about 20 of us, including some small children. The little ones were given a sleeping tablet so they wouldn't cry or make a noise. We got into the fishing boat at dawn the next day. The fisherman hid us under a big tarpaulin and we set off.

The journey across to Sweden usually took about two and a half hours, but that day it took ten because the fisherman had to keep stopping and throwing his nets out, pretending to be fishing. It was very cramped and uncomfortable and we could see lights shining from German boats. It was all very frightening. Fortunately, we arrived in Sweden safely.

Once we arrived, we were taken to a church hall that had been turned into dormitories. In another room that was like a canteen, we were given a bread roll and some tomato soup. I remember we were only allowed one roll and one bowl of soup because more boatloads of people were arriving through the day and night.

I didn't go to school for that first year in Sweden, but I learnt Swedish very quickly. After my baby sister was born in January 1944, I went to a nice Swedish school, where I was treated exceptionally well. We were the only refugee family living in the little town and the local people did a lot to help us. I remember there was a school skiing trip, but money was very tight at home so I didn't say anything about it. One day when I got to school, there was a weekend case on my desk. I put my hand up and said, "Excuse me, miss, there's a case on my desk." And the teacher said, "Yes, it's for you." I opened it and inside there were sweaters, socks and mittens – everything you needed for a winter break. I burst into tears and my teacher said, "Did you really think we'd go without you?" Then she gave me a little brown envelope and said, "This is from the teachers. It's your spending money – just the same as the other children."

We stayed in Sweden until 1945, the end of the war, then went back to Copenhagen. We were so happy to discover that all our family had survived. We went to see if our flat was still there. Our lovely neighbour – again non-Jewish – had even rented it out while we were away and kept the money for us.

Back in Copenhagen, I finished my schooling and met up with my old friends again. I desperately wanted to train to be a dress designer and work for the biggest fashion house in Copenhagen. I got an apprenticeship there and qualified as a cutter and designer when I was 18. Then I came to England in 1952, where I met and married my late husband, but that's another story...

I like to tell my story to schoolchildren because I think they can learn from my experiences. We live in a multi-racial society in England. We are lucky to live in a free country and should mix with everybody and try to understand other people's culture. Think what the wonderful Danish and Swedish people did for me and my family...

Blanche with her parents and baby sister, in Sweden, 1944

Harry, aged two, in Vienna, Austria, 1927

HARRY BIBRING

I couldn't speak a word of English

My name is Harry Bibring and I was born on 26 December 1925, in Vienna, Austria. My parents were both born in Poland, but they had met in Vienna. My mother was a lovely lady who came from a religious community in Poland. My father was less religious; he was a gentle man and very protective of his children. My sister, Gerta, was two years older than me.

We lived in a block of flats on a main road leading to the centre of Vienna. At home, we kept the Jewish religious festivals and had food that followed the special dietary rules.

As a child, I adored ice-skating. I learned to skate when I was five and spent most of my free time at the ice rink in Vienna. I always wanted to play ice hockey, but my father wouldn't let me because he was so protective.

I disobeyed him... until one day I was injured. Then my father got to know about it and I was given a good hiding! When I was little, my favourite toy was a teddy bear, but I had to leave it behind when I left Vienna.

When I was six, I went to primary school in Vienna, but I wasn't a very good student. I didn't work very hard. At the age of ten, you had to pass an exam to go to grammar school. If you didn't pass, you went to secondary school and left to go to work at 14. I didn't want to do that, so I decided I had to pass that exam. I started to work hard for the first time in my life – and I passed! But after that, I went back to my old ways... I know I gave my mother an unhappy time because I didn't really like anything at school.

Everything changed when I was 12, when Hitler occupied Austria. In my class, there were 13 Jewish children and about 20 non-Jewish children. We were all friends until that Friday – 11 March 1938. When I went back to school on the following Monday, there was a distinct barrier between the two groups. The non-Jewish children had obviously been told by their parents not to associate with the Jewish children. When we started a conversation with them, they just answered 'yes' or 'no', then turned away and talked to someone else. Later on, all the Jewish children were dismissed from the grammar school.

By 9 November 1938, the night we now call the

'Night of Broken Glass', things were really deteriorating for the Jews. It had all begun two days before when a Jewish man in Paris shot a German diplomat. I remember hearing on the radio that all the Jews would have to pay for this crime. My father was very scared. From our block of flats, we could see the smoke rising from the nearby synagogue that was on fire. Then the next day, my father was arrested. A few hours later, on 10 November, my mother, sister and I were collected by the Nazi police. First we were taken to the police headquarters and then to a flat, where there were about 50 Jewish ladies and children.

It was a terrible time because on top of everything else, I had developed appendicitis and was lying there in pain. My mother was worried to bits. It all lasted about ten days – probably the worst days of my mother's life. After that, we were allowed to go home. My father came back as well and told us he had been held in prison. His shop had also been a casualty of the violence. There was nothing left. All the stock had been stolen; all the mirrors and fittings broken.

After those frightening events, my parents decided that we had to emigrate. Many of our friends had already left, but we had no family in England or America who could help us get the right travel papers. My father told us that it was possible to go to Shanghai in China. He decided to sell all the valuables in the flat and my mother's jewellery to get the money for the tickets. But unfortunately, after he got the money, he was robbed and that possibility disappeared.

A few days later, my father heard about a scheme for children to leave Vienna on special trains called *Kindertransport* (Children's transport). He wanted my sister and me to go, and had found some people in England to take care of us. My parents were going to find a way of joining us as soon as possible.

My sister and I left Vienna on 13 March 1939. At the station, there were 600 children all saying goodbye to their parents; the crying was very sad to hear. I was 13, but many of the children were much younger. It was the first time we had been anywhere on our own.

The old-fashioned steam train travelled very slowly. We left at 10 p.m. and it took all night and the next day to reach Holland. There, the Dutch Jewish community gave us sweets, toys, food and clothes. The platforms were full of smiling people. They were the first friendly faces we had seen for a long time. Then we travelled overnight by ferry to Harwich in England, and arrived at Liverpool Street station, London, on 15 March.

When I arrived in England, my biggest problem was that I couldn't speak a word of English! Another blow came on the first evening when the people who had agreed to take care of us said they only had room for my sister. I was going to stay with one of their relatives. In fact, I was going to stay with lots of different relatives... The first was for two weeks, the second just a week. In the first few months I had eight different addresses! It was very unsettling.

When war broke out in September 1939, the whole of my school in London was evacuated to Peterborough. I was very fortunate because I lived with a headmaster who taught at the local grammar school. He developed my English a lot.

My sister was evacuated to Wales and we could only write letters to each other. We also wrote to our parents, but after the war started, there was no post and we had to write via friends in America. I actually have about 40 letters that we received from our parents like that – and in every one they said they were still trying to find a way of coming to England. In December 1940, one letter brought the news that my father had died of a heart attack after being arrested to go to a concentration camp.

It was a very sad period for me, but it also made me grow up. I turned 14 and started work for the first time – as an errand boy. After a year, I decided that I really wanted to be an engineer, so I got an apprenticeship and started going to night school. Eventually, against all the odds, I got two degrees in engineering; and I got married, had a lovely son and two gorgeous grandchildren. So something good came out of that terrible situation. But one of the saddest things was that my mother didn't live to see me make something of my life. She was rounded up by the Nazis in June 1942 and died in a concentration camp in Poland.

Because of my experiences, my son and grandchildren are all very aware of the dangers of racism and what they can lead to. They know that if you hear one person discriminate against another just because he is a different colour or follows a different religion, you have to stand up and say, "STOP!" If you don't, it can lead to what became the Holocaust.

Harry's father's shop in Vienna, which was ransacked in 1938

Harry with his parents and sister in Austria, 1927

Growing up in England, aged 14 in 1944

MARTHA BLEND

A child alone

My name is Martha Blend and I was born in 1930 in Vienna, the capital of Austria. My parents originally came from Poland, but they had met and married in Vienna. They were Jewish and we kept the main festivals, but they were not extremely religious. My father used to take me for walks in Vienna on Sundays. My mother was a very good cook and wanted me to have a good education. I was an only child, but my aunt and uncle lived nearby and I grew up with their two young children.

As a child, I enjoyed playing with my little Wendy House and with a lovely blonde doll that I brought to England with me. I also loved my school in Vienna, especially the singing. The teacher made me cupboard monitor and I was very proud to give out all the books. My best friend at school was called Grete. Her family were Catholic, but in those days it didn't make much difference. We were close friends until the Hitler times.

When the Germans invaded Austria in 1938, the atmosphere changed completely. My parents knew that we were in for a hard time. They had read in the newspaper how Hitler was treating the Jews of Germany and I had already picked up vibes of fear when the grown-ups mentioned names like "Hitler" and "Gestapo" (the Nazi secret police). My parents tried to emigrate to another country, but all the countries that could have taken us in were only allowing a trickle of refugees to enter. It would have been years before our turn came.

Life in Austria changed. Now, wherever you went, there were flags with swastikas and men in uniform with swastika armbands. Then a law was introduced which affected me personally: Jewish children had to be taught in separate classes. Suddenly, I was cut off from the teacher I loved and my schoolfriends, including Grete. I now had to go into school by a different door and found myself in a different classroom with a new teacher.

It was if our world had turned upside down. There were lots of restrictions for Jews – you couldn't sit on park benches or go to the cinema. The people you thought were your friends were no longer so and there was a terrible atmosphere of fear.

Then, in autumn 1938, came the horrible night of violence that we now call *Kristallnacht*, the 'Night of the Broken Glass'. In every town in Germany and Austria, synagogues were burned, shops owned by Jews smashed up and looted, homes broken into. Worst of all, thousands of Jewish men were arrested and sent to concentration camps. My father was one of those arrested and I can never forget the sound of Nazi boots stomping up our stairs and battering on the door. I was terrified.

My father was released after several weeks, but this experience made my parents search more desperately for a safe place to go to. They heard of an organisation called the *Kindertransport* (Children's transport), that had been set up to bring Jewish children to England as temporary refugees. When our doctor told my parents of a couple he knew in England who were willing to foster a child, they put me down on the list.

When they broke this news to me, I was devastated. I was an only child who had never been away from home and now I was going to travel to a strange country and to strange people with a different language! It seemed more than I could cope with at the age of nine, but things got so frightening that I knew I had to go.

A letter arrived, giving the date of my departure: we were told to assemble at a railway station in Vienna late on 20 June, bringing a small suitcase. Preparations for the journey now began in earnest. My mother found a small case which we packed with a few belongings: some underwear, a skirt and blouse, a dress and my most treasured possessions – my blonde doll, some pictures of my parents, my autograph book and some of my favourite reading-books.

By this time, my father had been arrested again and was in a police-prison in Vienna. The day before I was due to leave, my mother took me to see him. He looked sad and unshaven, very different from the smart man I had known as a little child. I don't remember much of what he said to me. He embraced me tenderly and wished me a safe journey. That was my last sight of my father.

I lived through the next day as though in a trance. My case was packed, I said goodbye to my aunt and cousins and promised to write to them. That evening, my mother took me to the station. When we arrived, there were already large numbers of children and their parents there. My mother and I kept to the rules we had been given: no emotional farewells. We managed not to cry. Suddenly, the big doors at the end of the waiting-room opened to reveal a platform with a train ready to be boarded. I embraced my mother for the last time. Then with a light suitcase, a heavy heart and a silly red hat that kept flopping into my face, I climbed into a compartment on the train. Suddenly, there was an outcry and a rush to the windows. Parents had been told that they must not follow their children onto the platform, but they were disobeying orders. They surged out of the waiting-room and onto the platform. Their children were able to wave a last goodbye. I scanned the sea of faces anxiously, hoping to have a last glimpse of my mother, but she wasn't there.

The train took us through Germany along the river Rhine and into Holland. There we boarded a ship bound for Harwich on the English east coast, and then another train, to Liverpool Street station, London. By that time I was so tired and bewildered after being very seasick on the boat. In London, we waited in a big room till our names were called out and we met the people who were going to look after us.

My foster mother took me to her home in Bow, in east London. The day after I arrived in England, I remember waking up in a strange bed in an unfamiliar room – and feeling very homesick. My foster mother did her best to comfort me. In England, everything was different. At home, we lived in a flat; now I lived in a house. The food was different and I had never had English tea before. And, of course, I had to speak English.

Later that year, the British Government ordered all London schoolchildren to be evacuated to the country. War was imminent and London was sure to be a target for German bombers. My foster mother evacuated herself and me to Paignton in Devon. After we had settled in, I was enrolled in the local primary school. I had learned a little English before leaving Austria, but not enough to fully grasp what people were saying. I remember this led to some funny misunderstandings when I was at school or playing with the other children. And some kids at school thought I was a German spy!

I came to England when I was nine, but when the war ended, I was fifteen. I had had no word from my parents for five years and was dreading finding out what had happened to them. I eventually learned the sad fact that my parents, along with my grandmothers, aunts, uncles and cousins, had all shared the fate of the millions of Jews who were murdered in Hitler's concentration camps and gas chambers.

There was nothing to go back to Austria for, so I made my home in this country and stayed with my foster parents until I got married. After I went to university, I spent 25 years as a teacher of English, my second language. Since my retirement, I have written a book about my experiences. I have also told my story to the pupils of many schools – to show how hate-propaganda can have terrible consequences and lead to murder. That is a lesson we dare not forget today.

Martha's story is told in full in *A Child Alone* (Vallentine Mitchell, London, 1995).

With my foster mother at the seaside, August 1939

Eva and her mother, Cardiff, 1950

Eva Clarke

Born in a concentration camp

My name is Eva Clarke and I was born in Austria in April 1945 – in a concentration camp called Mauthausen. I know that sounds very strange, so I want to tell you my story just as I heard it from my mother.

My parents, Bernd and Anka, met in Prague, Czechoslovakia, and were married in May 1940. My father was German, but went to live in Prague after Hitler came to power, hoping to be safe there. He was an architect/designer and till then had scarcely thought about the fact that he was Jewish. My mother is Czech. She was a university student in Prague, but when the Germans invaded Czechoslovakia, they shut down the Czech universities, so she found a practical job – as a trainee hat-maker.

My mother and father lived a fairly normal life in Prague for a year and a half, although the city was under

Nazi occupation. That meant there were all kinds of restrictions for Jews – a strict curfew, wearing the yellow star and not being allowed to go to parks, swimming pools and cinemas. In spite of this, I know my parents did sometimes take risks. Once, my mother was desperate to see a particular film, so she went to the cinema. But the Nazi police came in and started checking everyone's papers. Luckily, they stopped just one row in front of her, then left the cinema! She was so relieved that she never took a risk like that again!

This 'normal' life ended in December 1941 when my parents were sent to the town of Theresienstadt, which had been turned into a ghetto for Jews from all over Europe. My father left first, my mother a few days later. They were told to report to a warehouse in Prague, taking warm clothing and a few pots and pans for cooking. My mother also carried a large cardboard box containing doughnuts! She said you never knew where the next meal was coming from!

In Theresienstadt, my parents were part of a group whose job was to help set up the camp. The Nazis had apparently 'promised' that they would not be sent 'east', as was usual from there – to the death camps. They did remain in Theresienstadt for three years – much longer than most – because they were young and capable of hard work – and luck also had a lot to do with it.

My mother got a job in the camp working for the man responsible for sharing out the food. That meant she could sometimes steal a potato, carrot or turnip to supplement the normal watery soup. This helped her a lot because at one time she was trying to find enough food for 15 members of the family. My parents felt sure they would survive the war like this in Theresienstadt – and they decided to have a baby. My brother Jiri (George) was born in February 1944, but died from pneumonia two months later.

Their luck finally ran out in September 1944 when my father was sent to Auschwitz concentration camp. My mother had no idea where he had gone, but thought nothing could get much worse. She had no idea what Auschwitz was and imagined it would be like Theresienstadt. So next day, she actually *volunteered* to go there. But she never saw my father again. She found out much later that he had been shot in Auschwitz, just one week before the camp was liberated. My father never knew that she was pregnant again – with me.

My mother was in Auschwitz from 1-10 October 1944 and says it was "hell on earth". The journey there was terrifying – in a packed cattle truck without food or water and with a bucket for a toilet. When they arrived, they were confronted with Nazi guards screaming orders and vicious barking dogs. She couldn't make out what this place was.

The prisoners went though a first 'selection' to choose those who could work. Then their hair was shaved off, they were given striped uniforms and most people were tattooed with a number. This didn't happen to my mother – she doesn't know why. Then she was sent into one of the huts, totally bewildered.

Those ten days in Auschwitz were terrifying. Prisoners were registered twice a day, at 4.00 a.m. and 6.00 p.m. People had to stand outside their huts for hours and hours, in all weathers, to be counted. My mother fainted several times and when she came round, she was so relieved to find her friends holding her up.

After ten days, as my mother still looked capable of physical labour, she was sent to work in a weapons factory in Freiberg, Germany. On arrival, the prisoners had to cope with hundreds of bedbugs – on the floor, the walls, the ceiling! But after what they had been through in Auschwitz, that was nothing.

During my mother's six months in Freiberg, she became more and more starved and more obviously pregnant, but luckily the Germans never noticed. By this time, they were beginning to lose the war. The prisoners were delighted to witness the Allies' bombing raids on the nearby town of Dresden. They knew that help was coming.

Then the Germans started to evacuate the camps because they didn't want to leave living witnesses behind. At the beginning of April 1945, the prisoners from the Freiberg factory were put on another train – filthy open coal trucks – and they travelled round the countryside for three weeks without any food and hardly any water. Every day or so, the train would stop in the middle of the countryside. One time, my mother was standing by the door when a farmer walked by. He was stunned to see this starved, pregnant woman and brought her a glass of milk. She normally hates milk, but she reckons that drink saved our lives – who knows?

The train moved on and arrived in Mauthausen, Austria, a beautiful alpine village on the banks of the River Danube. This time my mother did know what the name Mauthausen meant – a terrible concentration camp – and she was so shocked that her labour pains started.

I was born weighing about 3 lb/1.5 kg, like a bag of sugar. I had lots of dark brown hair and was wrapped in paper – obviously there were no baby clothes. How on earth did I survive? Well, there were a few pieces of luck. A Nazi officer saw that my mother was in labour, but left her alone. A prisoner who was a doctor cut the cord and smacked me to make me cry – and breathe. And three days later, the Americans liberated the camp. My mother says that we wouldn't have survived much longer without help.

Three weeks later, once we were strong enough, we were sent back to Prague. We arrived on a dark, dismal night, my mother still in her prison uniform, but by then I had been given some baby clothes. We made our way to my aunt Olga's flat, where my mother asked if we could stay for a few days to recover. We actually stayed there for three years until my stepfather, Karel Bergman, came on the scene and they got married in 1948. Then we left Czechoslovakia to start a new life in Cardiff.

So that is how my life began in Mauthausen concentration camp...

Eva and her mother at the Holocaust Centre, Nottinghamshire, 21 April 2002
(the day after Anka's 85th birthday)

Hans as a toddler at the seaside in Germany

HANS COHN

I lost the sight of one eye

My name is Hans Cohn and I was born in May 1923, in Berlin, Germany. My father's name was George and my mother's Lucy. My father was a solicitor and had very good connections – some of his clients were well-known people in the acting profession. He was very proud to have fought for Germany in the First World War. My mother was from an average German Jewish family, but her father was originally from Poland. He started a factory when he moved to Berlin and was the first to produce plastic buttons in Germany in the 1920s. My parents were married in 1921; my father was 36 and my mother 20.

My father used to go to the synagogue on Friday nights at the beginning of the Sabbath, but he wasn't strictly religious and went to work in his office on Saturdays. He observed all the high holidays and we always had a special family meal on Fridays. I can still remember the blessing for the wine and bread – it's the only bit of Hebrew I remember after all these years. We usually had people with us for dinner – relatives or people who lived alone. We had a normal meal of fish or meat; we didn't keep all the Jewish rules about food, but we didn't eat pork.

We lived in quite a large house, divided into flats. When you went in the front door, the lift was facing you and there were corridors to the right and left. The house had four or five floors, so there were about ten flats altogether. Our flat had two bedrooms, a dining room, a study (it was called the 'gentleman's room') and a sitting room, as well as a kitchen and maid's room. It was a normal middle-class home, nothing too opulent.

I don't remember much about my very early life, except what I was told afterwards. One of my earliest memories is about cod liver oil, which in those days children took every day to make them fit and strong. One day, when I was very small, I drank a whole bottle!

As a child, I remember playing with a wind-up train and I was always very interested in animals. We didn't have any pets ourselves, but most of our relatives had dogs. Later on, when I went to school, I had to pass Berlin Zoo on my way home and I was given a season ticket for my birthday. I particularly liked the tigers and elephants – the elephants played instruments in a little orchestra and it was quite amazing! I made friends with some of the animals because I used to go every day. Eventually, the keepers let me into the tiger and lion cages to watch them being fed. I was quite fearless then!

My primary school was private and not very far from home. When I was 10, in September 1933, I moved to a non-Jewish secondary school. By then Hitler was in power and I was only allowed to go there because my father had been a soldier in the First World War. It was a special school called a French *lycée* (grammar school) and French was taught from the first form. A lot of the pupils were the children of diplomats in Berlin. The classes were fairly small and I think we had about six Jewish children in the class. My favourite subjects were French, Latin and History. One big change in 1933 was that some of the teachers came to school wearing Nazi uniforms.

I wasn't treated unfairly at school because I was Jewish. Obviously, there was a division among my classmates and some supported Hitler and all he stood for. I kept away from them, but we didn't actually fight. One of the boys in my class was the son of a Nazi party official. He was the one who caused my blindness.

One day, we were all sitting in our places in the hall and next to me there was a Jewish friend of mine. Another boy, who was in the Hitler Youth movement, started fighting my neighbour because he wanted to move seats, but unfortunately he hit me by accident. My eye was seriously injured. My parents found a specialist in Holland and I had two operations, both unsuccessful. It was the most terrifying experience of my childhood because I had no anaesthetic and I couldn't understand a word people were saying. That's how I lost the sight of one eye.

Because the incident happened at school, the headmaster felt responsible and I was allowed to continue my education there, whereas normally in those days I would have had to go to a special school. About a year later, I also lost the sight in my second eye from a kind of infection. That changed my life completely. I lost my friends because I couldn't really play games with them, and my visits to the zoo stopped because I couldn't go on my own. By this time it was 1936 and conditions for Jews had deteriorated over the years, but I was never actually molested. I think that was probably partially due to my blindness.

I learned to type and use Braille at home, and my school work took a lot of my time. I went to school by underground train. My father took me to the station and I met a boy there who then took me to school. The same thing happened on the way back. So I had lost my independence.

Later on, my parents decided I would have to go abroad because I wasn't being taught the skills I needed for a useful life as a blind person. That's why I came to England – not really because of the problems for Jews in Germany. In fact, they tried to get me into the best school for the blind in Germany, but Jewish boys were not allowed to go there. My mother heard about Worcester College for the Blind and that's where I went in May 1938.

My mother and I travelled overnight via Holland and we spent a couple of days in London with friends from Berlin who had emigrated two years earlier. Then my mother took me to Worcester and left me at the boarding school. I'd already started English lessons, but couldn't speak very well. Communication was difficult. I could speak French when the French teacher was there, but he wasn't resident at school. Otherwise, I remember speaking in Latin to the Classics master!

I went back to Berlin for the summer holidays in 1938, but then my mother wrote to tell me I couldn't go back to Germany at Christmas because I might not be able to leave again. So I spent Christmas with a schoolfriend. By the next holiday, Easter 1939, my mother was already in London. She had found a position working in one of the homes where refugee children were looked after.

Before war broke out, my mother tried to get my father out of Germany, but he stayed because he could pay my school fees from there. Then the war came and it was impossible to leave. He was eventually deported in 1941 and we heard from the Red Cross in 1942 that he had died as a result of a medical operation. I was still at school and one of the teachers told me.

After school, I went to London and lived in the hostel for refugees where my mother was matron. I trained as a physiotherapist. I was lucky because physiotherapy was very much in demand after the war with all the injured servicemen and civilians who needed treatment. I've learnt to be as independent as I can and not let my blindness interfere with normal activities. I've made the best of my life.

I lost the sight of one eye

Hans with his guide dog

Nicole, aged three, 1939

NICOLE DAVID

Growing up in hiding

I was born in Antwerp, Belgium, in September 1936,
the only daughter of Chawa and Munisch Schneider.
My mother and father were originally from Poland, but
they had moved to Belgium in the 1920s. They both
came from a religious background and I remember my
mother teaching me the most important Jewish prayers,
which I used to say every night.

As a little girl, I have happy memories of my mother
teaching me to swim in the river in the little village
where we lived, and my father reading me bedtime
stories about Mickey Mouse. I remember my mother
telling me off for eating too many sugar lumps. I could
easily eat 30 in one go! And I remember going to visit
our neighbours' rabbits at the bottom of the garden.
But behind all these memories lies an atmosphere of
fear – because I was only a little girl of four when the

Nazis invaded on 10 May 1940. This event changed my childhood years completely.

Over the first two years of Nazi occupation, various laws were passed restricting the freedom and movement of Jews. We weren't allowed to run our own businesses, and cinemas, theatres and parks were all out of bounds. I wasn't even supposed to go to school, but a nun let me go to nursery for a while. By May 1942, Jews had to wear a yellow star – except for children under six. I can still remember German soldiers inspecting my parents' coats to make sure the star was sewn on properly.

By August 1942, my parents were really worried about our safety because the Nazis had started sending people away to concentration camps. They decided we would have to go into hiding, but couldn't find a place that would take all three of us. I was put into a Catholic orphanage run by nuns and my parents hid in an attic and were protected by a Belgian family.

I was very unhappy in the orphanage. I was only six. It was the first time I had been separated from my parents and I kept on getting tonsillitis, so the orphanage couldn't keep me because of the risk of infection for the other children. Antibiotics didn't exist then. I needed to have my tonsils out.

There was no choice: we had to go back to where we lived before we went into hiding. We planned to stay one week so I could have my tonsils out. Then, once I was better, I was going to be hidden by another family that my mother had found.

I was so happy to be home. The day before the operation, 7 October 1942, I went out to buy a newspaper with my father while my mother was preparing lunch. It was a beautiful day and we stopped for a while at a café by the river. I was even allowed to have a sip of my father's drink! But when we got near to home again, we saw three German lorries in front of the house. I never saw my mother again.

Luckily, some members of the Belgian Resistance helped my father and me to escape. They knew what had happened and were waiting to take us to a safe house. We spent the rest of the day there while the Germans were searching for us. Later that evening, the members of the Resistance took my father back to the attic where he had been hiding, and I was taken to stay with Monsieur and Madame Champagne. They were Catholics, the parents of a neighbour my mother had made friends with. They had ten children, five still at home. The Champagne family took me in, knowing full well that they were risking the lives of their whole family. They pretended I was Madame Champagne's niece, but they could all have been killed for hiding a Jew.

I lived with them for one and a half years and was treated as one of the family. They never took any money for keeping me. My only outing was going to church with the family, and for me this was a great treat.

My mother had asked them to remind me to say the Jewish prayers she had taught me, and so every evening their daughter, Paulette, would make sure I didn't forget. I didn't go to school because questions from other children might have been dangerous. I was by myself most of the time. I was very lonely. Every day I spent hours and hours making up fantasy stories about an imaginary friend called Mickey. I wasn't a loner by nature. I loved company and chatting, but I had to become very independent. I learned to live day by day and not to think too much, but I really missed the warmth of my parents.

I remember that I was given a special treat on my seventh birthday. I was allowed to go out for a walk with Yvonne, a German Jewish girl who had been with us since 1938. She had blond hair and blue eyes and was working locally, using false identity papers. While I was waiting for her, I wandered off on my own. Before I realized, I had walked right to the other end of the village – and the whole family was out looking for me! I can still remember my punishment. I had to write out 250 times "I am not allowed to go out alone."

After about one and a half years, I was separated from the Champagne family because there was a risk of bombing nearby. I was moved to a farm in another village. Very soon after my arrival, some Germans drove up to the farm where I was staying. As soon as I saw the car coming, I ran to my room, got into bed and pretended to be ill. Fortunately, they weren't interested in me. They were looking for the farmer's two sons because they wanted to send them to work in Germany. After that, I was moved on and hidden again. It was too dangerous for me to stay in that village.

By then, there were rumours that the Americans were coming to set us free. The rumours were true and we were liberated on 6 September 1944. An American soldier jumped down from his lorry to give me a bar of chocolate. I was so frightened by his uniform that I ran away. When the family I was staying with caught up with me, they explained that this was a friendly uniform. It was all very confusing for a little girl of eight.

I was eventually reunited with my father, but we soon had to move again because there was still a lot of fighting happening. So we went to Brussels and stayed there till the end of the war. Even then, we were separated again because we didn't have a home where we could be together. This time I was put in a convent, where I was looked after by Christian nuns. Although my father came to see me nearly every day, this last separation was really difficult for me because I had been told the Germans had gone and I wanted things to be normal again. Eventually, after all the chaos, normal life did resume – but tragically, without many of our loved ones.

When I look back today at those years spent in hiding, I can remember being frightened and bewildered by what was happening. But I also realise now how many people put their own lives at risk to save my father and me. It shows us how much goodness there was amongst all that evil. It helps us to remember that individual people can make a tremendous difference.

Nicole, aged three, with her mother in Antwerp Park, winter 1939

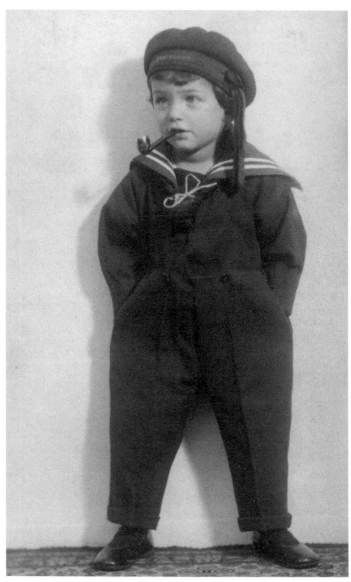

Manfred pretending to be a sailor, early 1930s

MANFRED DESSAU

It could so easily have been me

My name is Manfred Dessau and I was born on 9 August 1926 in Leipzig, Germany. My father, Victor, and my mother, Regina, were both born in Poland, but their families had emigrated to Germany in the early 1910s. My older brother, Joe, was born in 1923. I have clear memories of those early years in Leipzig. I remember the two houses we lived in before we went to stay with my grandfather's family.

By the time of this last move, my father had already left Germany in rather a hurry, in July 1934. He had little choice because he was due to appear in court over a driving offence. For a Jew, this would certainly have meant being sent to a prison, and later a concentration camp. My father was also afraid of what might happen in Germany with the rapid rise of the Nazi Party. He was only able to leave because he could obtain a Polish passport. He travelled to England, but had to leave his wife and two sons behind.

Life was hard for us in those months in Germany, without Father to take care of us. Like all Jewish children after 1933, Joe and I were forced to leave the local school and transfer to a Jewish one. I remember the day Adolf Hitler visited Leipzig and the huge crowds lining the streets as he stood in his car. People raised their arms and screamed *"Heil Hitler"* at the tops of their voices.

Finally, Mother, Joe and I made it to England – and again it was because my mother was able to get a Polish passport with our names on it. We left Leipzig on 1 November 1935, travelling by train to the Hook of Holland and then by boat to Harwich. We arrived there on 2 November and then went by train to London. We were met at the station by our cousins, Zonia and Helen Dessau.

I remember little or nothing of those first 24 hours in London, but I can't forget my excitement at the next train journey – from London to Victoria Station in Nottingham. The train had hardly stopped before I jumped out into my father's arms. Mother and Father were both crying on the station platform – tears of joy and relief. Another cousin, Heinz, took us to a rented house, our first home in Great Britain – Number 2A,

Burnham Street, Sherwood, Nottingham. Our first meal there was prepared by Heinz and it was actually beans on toast!

Our second day in Nottingham was 5 November. Our house at Number 2A was next to an open piece of land, where we played and made friends later on. But on that day, there was an enormous bonfire and lots of fireworks. It's difficult to describe how Joe and I reacted to that wonderful display. Believe it or not, we really thought it was a welcome celebration for our family!

Soon after we arrived, my father talked to us about our future in our new country. I remember him saying very clearly, "We're in England now, so we'll speak English and be English." Of course, it didn't mean that we wouldn't be Jewish, or we couldn't go to synagogue. But it meant that we should mix with our neighbours in Sherwood and make friends with them.

My father already spoke good English and it wasn't a great problem for Joe and me to learn. But my mother didn't go to work or school, so it was much more difficult for her.

I remember clearly that for one of our first family meals in Burnham Street, there was butter on the table. This seemed amazing to us because Jews in Germany, even in 1935, were only allowed to buy margarine. And in case you're wondering how the shopkeepers knew we were Jews, we had to wear a yellow Star of David on our outer clothes.

Joe and I started at Haydn Road Primary School, just a short way from home. Everyone was very friendly there – even if we were a bit of a curiosity! I went to school wearing knickerbockers (knee-length trousers) and a round hat with a pompom! We didn't speak a word of English at first, but one teacher knew a few words of German. Going to school helped us to learn English quickly – and with a good Nottingham accent! Within a few months, Joe and I were quite fluent and had no difficulty with our lessons. We soon made friends and the other children realised we weren't really any different from them.

After primary school, Joe went to Claremont School and I passed the entrance exam for High Pavement Grammar, in 1937. That was quite a different school and I was definitely looked upon as 'the foreigner' – but not in a cruel way. I wasn't a very brilliant student but I was a member of the Junior Rugby team. Rather than being bullied myself, I am ashamed to admit that for a while I was one of the school bullies. Very soon, my Housemaster had me in his office and reminded me why I was in England and at this school. It was a very sobering 15 minutes. My bullying days were over.

1937 was a very important year for our family. Our sister Faye was born, and my father was offered the chance to start a factory making men's dressing gowns. He was really thrilled and called it Burnham Manufacturing after our street. I also started to go to *Cheder* school – that's Sunday School, if you like – and started lessons for my Bar mitzvah or confirmation classes. While I was at *Cheder*, on Sunday 3 September 1939, I heard the announcement on the wireless, "This country is now at war with Germany."

Only two weeks after war broke out – I was then just 13 – all the pupils of High Pavement School were evacuated to Mansfield, just 15 miles from Nottingham. I was uprooted again. But this evacuation to Mansfield only lasted about 18 months. By early 1941, I was living back at home.

During the war years, in Mansfield and back at home, we had to work on farms during the summer holidays to help with the war effort. I also joined the "Civil Defence Cadet Corps". It meant that if we had bicycles, we could run errands and deliver messages for the Air Raid Wardens. Someone in the Cadet Corps found out I could speak German. Very soon, I was asked to interpret for German prisoners of war as they arrived in Nottingham. It wasn't really interrogation – more practical questions about their personal needs.

I left High Pavement School in 1942, at the age of 16, and got a job as an electrician's mate. Why an electrician's mate? My father had very strong views about careers for his sons. We had to have jobs that could be done anywhere in the world. Having been forced to flee to a new life in a different country, he thought that as an electrician, plumber or mechanic of any sort, you would get a job wherever you were. As a doctor or lawyer, you would arrive in a new country and have to start all over again. Later on, I joined my father at his clothing company... and so began a career that was to last for 40 years.

It could so easily have been me

Manfred enjoying skating in the early days of Nottingham Ice Rink

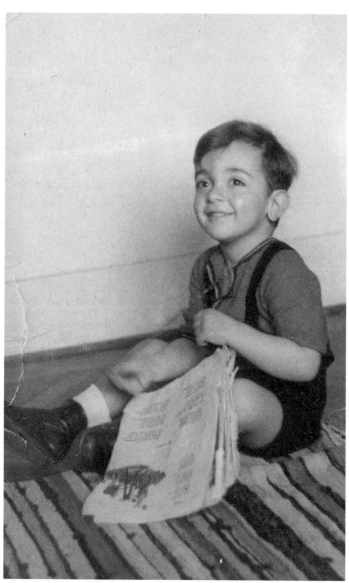

John, aged three, at home in Budapest

JOHN DOBAI

Saved by Raoul Wallenberg

My name is John Dobai and I was born on 6 January 1934 in Budapest, the capital of Hungary. I was an only child. My father worked in a bank and was a very keen sportsman. In the 1920s, he had an Olympic trial for the Hungarian athletics team. He was a good skier and played football for a Second Division team. My mother was very good with textiles and I remember her weaving at her loom in our sitting room. We lived in a flat in a nice suburb of Budapest.

When I was young, we did a lot of walking in the spring and autumn. In the summer, we went swimming and rowing on the river, and in the winter, we went skiing. My father was particularly good at tennis and tried to teach me. I remember that he used to shout, "Don't pat the ball! Hit it!" Unfortunately, I wasn't nearly as good as my father!

My grandparents were very observant Jews who went to the synagogue. But my parents left religion behind and our immediate family and friends didn't go to the synagogue. We didn't consider ourselves Jewish. My parents thought it was likely that some anti-Jewish laws were going to be made, so I was christened a Roman Catholic. I grew up going to church and, as far as I knew, I was a Catholic.

I started school in 1940, when I was six, and found it very exciting. About the same time, my father was called up to the army when Hungary joined the Second World War. But he came back a few weeks later because the Hungarian Government didn't want any Jewish people in the army. Early in 1942, he was called up for work in a labour camp, where people had to build airfields and roads for the German Army. So I didn't see my father from 1942 until 1944.

I went to a Catholic school, so we went to church every Sunday and I served as an altar boy. I remember feeling uncomfortable when some anti-Jewish things were said in school – comments that some of Hungary's problems were actually due to the Jews. This was because my parents had told me never to speak badly about anyone who was somehow different.

Things changed dramatically after the Germans marched into Hungary. One day during the holiday, I met a boy from my class and said how much I was looking forward to going back to school. He told me that *he* would be going back to school, but I wouldn't. "Why shouldn't I go?" I asked.

"Because you're a stinking Jew."

"No I'm not, I'm a Roman Catholic."

"No, my father told me you're a stinking Jew."

I rushed back home to my mother and told her what had happened, and she had to explain it all to me. That was how I discovered my Jewish origins when I was about eight years old.

The war had been going very badly for Hungary and they were talking about perhaps making a separate peace with the British and Americans. When the Germans heard this, they came and occupied Hungary – bringing the dreaded Gestapo secret police with them. A lot of laws were brought in against the Jews; they had to give up their money, cars, bicycles, and so on. And they had to start wearing a yellow star to show they were Jewish. Now, if your parents or grandparents were Jewish, you were also considered a Jew. Although I'd been christened a Roman Catholic, I was now regarded as a Jew. It was humiliating to wear a yellow star. When you met somebody on the street who wasn't wearing one, you had to step off the pavement and walk in the gutter.

The Germans started rounding up all the Jews from the countryside and sending them to the concentration camp of Auschwitz. Then they started collecting up all the Jews of Budapest. Mother and I had to move from one place to another. We were told to gather our possessions together and stand in a line outside the house. I was ten years old. People lined the road to watch and some anti-Jewish Hungarians dashed out and snatched a nice duvet or a pillow as we passed. The soldiers didn't do anything about it. One of these people came up to me and shouted something about 'dirty rotten Jew' in my face. It was very frightening.

The situation had become very dangerous for us in Budapest. In the meantime, my father had been able to come back from the labour camp. He went to the Swedish embassy in Budapest and managed to obtain special Swedish passports for us. A diplomat called Raoul Wallenberg had come to Hungary specially to try and help people who were in danger of being killed by the Nazis.

With these passports, we moved about three kilometres to a special 'safe' house bought by the Swedish Government. It was a frightening journey because we had to cross the river Danube, where we were exposed to bullets, bombs and shells, and also there were several checkpoints with guards and soldiers who examined our papers. My parents told me not to say a word. Luckily, the guards accepted our documents.

I felt very much safer when the gates of the new house were shut behind us. I remember that we all cried with relief. We lived in a room on the top floor of that house. There was no glass in the windows, no heat, gas, electricity or water. There was no means of cooking and we were only occasionally able to get hold of food like potatoes or vegetables. My mother made soup with whatever she could, and I was responsible for smashing up furniture to keep the fires going. But – most important of all – the house had the Swedish flag outside, which protected us to some extent from the Nazis.

We managed to survive the harsh winter of 1944-45, with the war literally happening in the streets outside. It was a question of who would reach our house first. Would it be the Russians, to save our lives? Or the Nazis who were still intent on killing us? We remained there until 13 January 1945 when suddenly a Russian soldier appeared after a long period of house-to-house fighting. My father could speak Russian and explained that we were not Germans, we were not Nazis; we had suffered from them as well.

Thankfully, it was the Russian Army who arrived first – and that was how our family managed to survive.

We came to England in 1948 and my father said, "We don't know what the British people's attitude is towards Jews, so it might be best not to talk about it."

So I went to a Church of England church and in fact became a Sunday school teacher. But after the age of 17 I left religion behind, although I still believe strongly in human beings helping one another. We are all human beings and it is our duty to try and stop all cruelty and harm to others. When children come across anybody being unkind to another person – whether it's bullying in the playground or calling someone names because they are different in some way – they should tell that person it is the wrong thing to do.

John, aged seven, enjoying the snow in Budapest, 1941

John, aged one, 1932

JOHN FIELDSEND

Rescued by an Englishman

My name is John Fieldsend and I was born on 11 September 1931 in Czechoslovakia. My mother was Czech and my father was German from the town of Dresden. My mother had moved to Dresden to study photography and she had met my father there. My older brother was born in Dresden, but I was born in Czechoslovakia at my grandparents' home, although we moved back to Dresden later.

We were a happy family. We always had real winters with snow and we used to go sledging. I loved playing with a toy that was like Meccano, making model cars and so on. And we had a lovely black dog.

Religion wasn't very important in my upbringing. I think my father went to the synagogue about once a year, but I don't remember going at all. I think my parents already had quite strong Christian leanings because I remember far more about Easter and Christmas than about the Jewish festivals.

My earliest memories go back to the mid-1930s. I remember that Hitler paid a visit to Dresden in 1935 or 1936. Although we didn't go into the city centre, I can still hear Hitler's voice echoing in my head, "*Die Juden, die Juden, die Juden* – those terrible Jews". When I was five, my father was tickling me one day and I hit my head on the radiator. I had to go to the doctor's because I had cut my head. I remember the doctor said, "That needs a stitch, but I don't stitch Jews." So he put a plaster on it and today I've got a scar on my forehead.

There were other incidents like this. My parents were friendly with a non-Jewish German family who had boys the same age as us, and we used to play together. I remember them suddenly turning round one day, spitting and calling us "dirty Jews". I was only five and I remember feeling bewildered because I didn't understand what was odd about being Jewish. On another occasion, we were playing with children from the flats where we lived. Suddenly, they started calling us names and I remember my brother running into our flat to bring out the Iron Cross medal that my father had won in the First World War. He wanted to show that we were loyal Germans and Jewish.

Incidents like these made my parents decide to leave Dresden. One night, we left our flat, got into the car and drove to my grandparents' house in Czechoslovakia, where we thought we would be safe. It was a lovely home. There were four generations living in the same house – my brother and I, our parents, our grandparents and great-grandparents.

Our happy and secure life there lasted until Hitler occupied part of Czechoslovakia – before invading the rest of the country. Then all the troubles started again. One day, my father was in the garden cutting down a diseased fruit tree and a Nazi officer walked in and said, "Why are you cutting that tree down?" I think he thought we were just doing deliberate damage. I remember standing next to my father in the garden while he endured a full Nazi interrogation. I was still only five.

Things got very bad again until one day my father called my brother and me and said, "You're going on a long journey to a country called England. We can't come with you, but maybe when the troubles are over, you'll come back here or we'll come to you." He taught me to say, "I can't speak English" and those were the only English words I knew.

Shortly afterwards, our parents put us on a train and said goodbye. We had just one suitcase each with a few clothes and toys. We went first to a Jewish boarding school in Hanover, Germany, and stayed there for a couple of months. Then, one day, some of the staff took us to Hanover station and we were put on a children's transport train (*Kindertransport*) that had departed from Prague.

We arrived in England at the end of June 1939. I remember the ferry across the North Sea because I had never seen the sea before. We were met in London by my foster parents, who took me and my brother back to Sheffield. My foster father was deputy-manager of a big coal mine in Sheffield and they were a practising Christian family. They had a son who was seven months older than me. My brother went to a different family, not far from mine, and later became a respected doctor in Sheffield.

I think my earliest memories of England were of going to bed. I couldn't work out how to get into bed between sheets and blankets because I had never seen anything but continental quilts. I also remember double-decker buses in London and Sheffield. I thought they would topple over. And I was frightened of the open fire in the sitting room because we had stoves for heating at home.

I learnt English very quickly because my foster parents made sure that if I didn't ask for something in English, then I didn't get it. I soon learnt the names of English foods! I started school in September 1939, just two months after coming to England, and I don't remember having any language problems. But I forgot my German just as quickly. Later on, when I tried to learn German at school, I came bottom of the class!

It was a wonderful foster home and I was very happy there. In fact, I stayed until I got married in 1961. But Sheffield was blitzed by the German Air Force and so I was evacuated to another foster home in Bedford until the blitz was over. Now I was an evacuee as well as a refugee.

I got good results at school and then went to Nottingham University to study electrical engineering and electronics. My foster parents made sure I had a good education. After I'd been at work for a while, I decided to go back to studying and became an Anglican Church minister. By this time, I was more British than the British and had forgotten my Jewish roots completely. I suddenly woke up one morning and thought, "I'm Jewish. How on earth did I get here?" Today, I'm still a Christian and very much a Jewish believer in Jesus. I mix very happily in Jewish and Christian circles.

One day after the war, in 1946, I remember receiving three big family photo albums via the Red Cross, along with a letter from our parents. We hadn't heard from them since 1942. At first, I looked at the letter and thought, "They're alive!" But then I read it and realised that they had died. It was a very sad moment. The letter said, *"We want to say farewell to you, who were our dearest possessions in the world... We want you to become good men and think of our happy years together. We are going into the unknown... Don't forget us, and be good."*

I found out later that they had been deported to Poland in February 1943. Since then, I've been doing a lot of family research and I found out about the Englishman called Nicholas Winton who had rescued me – and more than 600 other children – on the *Kindertransport*. Without his bravery, I wouldn't be here today.

John's first day at school in Dresden, carrying the traditional cone of sweets, 1935

Dorli (Dorothy), aged six, 1934

DOROTHY FLEMING

All of a sudden the atmosphere changed

I was born Dorli Oppenheimer in 1928 in Vienna, Austria, and I was almost ten years old when Hitler joined Austria onto Germany. Several generations of our family had lived in Vienna. We lived in a big flat and my father owned two optician's shops. He was also very good at telling jokes and doing magic tricks! My mother was a very active lady: she sang in a choir, played the violin and did dancing and gymnastics.

I lived a very happy life with my parents and younger sister. I loved reading, dancing, gymnastics and helping with the cooking, and at weekends we used to go swimming, skiing, ice-skating and walking in the woods. I had a fantastic rocking horse with a real mane and tail, and I particularly remember the marvellous birthday parties that my mother organised. We had our own little puppet theatre and she used to put on a Punch and Judy show for us. I loved languages and had private English lessons from the age of seven – but I'm sure my parents had no idea how important this would turn out to be!

My family was Jewish, but not particularly religious; we didn't go to the synagogue regularly, but I remember going with my grandfather at special festival times. We had both Jewish and non-Jewish friends.

When Hitler came into Austria in 1938, I was already at High School and I was planning to study there until I went to university. But things started to change. First of all, the teacher made all the Jewish pupils, including me, sit at the back of the class, facing the wall. Then she told the other girls not to speak to us. Up to then, no one had paid any special attention to our religion. This sudden separation was hurtful and hard to understand. After a short time, she told the girls to listen carefully at home and report any nasty remarks they overheard. She was making children spy on their families. Then, after summer 1938, Jewish children were no longer allowed to attend ordinary schools and my education stopped.

There was even a change in the atmosphere at home. Grim faces seemed to replace smiles; silence took over from noise and laughter. The talk was all about permits and visas, people who had managed to escape, and what we would do now that the Nazis had taken over Daddy's shops.

At about this time, when everything was looking black and hopeless, my parents got to hear about the *Kindertransport*, the special trains that would take children to safety in England. I can imagine that my parents had endless discussions before they decided to send us. Many years later, I found out that a wonderful lady called Tilly Hall had offered to take in a girl of about ten who could speak a bit of English. But when she saw the photo of my little sister, Lisi, she apparently said, "Well, I really can't bear the idea of these two girls being separated from their parents as well as from each other... We'll take them both." And that was how Lisi and I came to England on the *Kindertransport* train and stayed in Leeds with Mr and Mrs Hall.

I remember being taken to say goodbye to family and friends. And I remember my parents explaining it all to me, saying we were going stay with a kind family in Leeds where I would have a chance to practise my English and take care of Lisi. And, of course, my parents said they would see us again soon.

I was really looking forward to this adventure. I'd been away from home before and was very independent and grown-up for my age. So, on 10 January 1939, when I was ten and a half and Lisi just four and a half, we went to the railway station in Vienna with our parents, taking one piece of luggage each (all that we were allowed). I took a little leather wallet with me containing a picture of my mother and father, as well as my precious autograph book. I remember there were lots of families on the platform and lots of noise. We were lucky that day because our parents were allowed to come on the platform. Later on, parents had to leave their children outside the station. That must have made it even worse. Our parents saw us into the compartment and said, "Bye bye. Be good girls and we'll be together again soon." Then they left.

After everyone's parents had gone, those of us who were older began to try and organise ourselves. There were two little ones among us: Lisi and one other. We decided to put them both up in the net luggage rack because we thought they might go to sleep there. But as soon as Lisi got up there, she was terribly sick. That kept me busy for the next half hour and it was probably a good thing. I can't actually remember the train leaving – lucky again!

After the train set off, messages started to come from other compartments warning us to be careful when we got to the border. We weren't supposed to have anything valuable with us, and if anything forbidden was found, or our papers were not in order, there could be big trouble. But we were lucky again; nothing awful happened to us during the inspection.

I remember very clearly arriving in Holland. There were lots of ladies dressed in black standing on the platform as the train drew in. They were all smiling as they welcomed us, offering us orange juice or hot chocolate and sweet buns. Their smiles were the best; it was ages since we'd seen people smiling.

The English Channel was a bit choppy, but luckily Lisi and I weren't seasick. I can't really remember arriving in London, but we were met at the station, then stayed overnight at an aunt's house. Next morning, we were taken back to the station and travelled to Leeds on our own.

My first memory of Leeds is arriving at Mr and Mrs Hall's house: 3 Garmont Road, Chapeltown, Leeds. Uncle Theo and Auntie Tilly were lovely people – young, smiley and loving, and they had a dog! A golden retriever called Buster who became my friend straight away. All my dreams were coming true. I'd always longed to live in a house, not a flat, and I'd always wanted a dog. The only problem was Lisi, my unhappy little sister – she had never been away from our parents before. She couldn't speak any English and didn't understand what people were saying to her. She cried and clung to me and would not be comforted. She even went back to wetting her bed. It took her a very long time to settle, but eventually she did. Then she forgot all her German and had to relearn it later!

For me, being in Leeds was great. I enjoyed going to school, especially all the 'fun' things I'd never done at school in Vienna – like gym, drama, art and craft. No one made me feel bad about being a foreigner or a Jew. And Theo and Tilly were the best foster parents you could wish for. They invited friends over to play with us and took us on outings. Perhaps most importantly, they helped us keep in touch with our parents and never tried to make us forget them. I was so lucky to be with a young, kind and Jewish couple. Luckiest of all, my parents also escaped to England four months after us, although we couldn't be together as a family for another two years because of my father's work.

Eventually, we were all reunited in Cardiff and I could at last get on with being a normal teenager. Because the war was still on, when I was 16 I became an 'enemy alien', which meant I had to report regularly to the police. I was hurt by this because by then I felt completely English! Later, I studied to become a teacher and met and married my husband, a doctor. He was also from Vienna, but had escaped from Hitler in a very different way. We went on to have three children, six grandchildren and four great-grandchildren.

So you can see that I was lucky many times over – especially because most of the *Kindertransport* children who came to England never saw their parents again.

Dorli (Dorothy), aged eight, on holiday in Millstadt, Austria, 1936

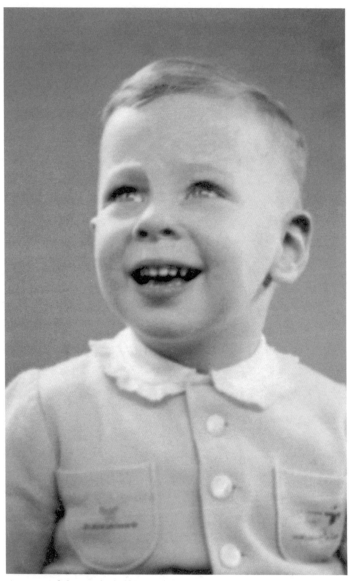

Steven, aged three and a half, December 1938

STEVEN FRANK

A second chance to live

My name is Steven Frank and I was born in Amsterdam, in the Netherlands, on 27 July 1935. My father was Dutch and a well known and successful lawyer. My mother was born in Eastbourne in England and had met and married my father in Amsterdam. They had three sons and I was the middle one.

We lived in a three-storied house in a smart part of Amsterdam that had been built for the Olympic Games in 1928. It was a very modern house for the time with a garage and central heating – and we even had a children's swing installed in the loft! As a child, I used to play a lot with my younger brother. We were a bit boisterous and one day he pushed me off the shed roof and I broke my wrist. I also remember distinctly being told off for picking our pet rabbit up by the ears.

I was nearly five years old when the Nazis marched into Amsterdam, but I didn't really understand what it meant. My father knew what might happen to the Jews of Holland. He joined the Dutch Resistance and was responsible for issuing false papers to help desperate Jews get out of the country. One morning in January 1943, he kissed us all goodbye and walked to his office in the centre of Amsterdam. I never saw him again.

We went into hiding briefly, but nothing happened to our house, so we returned. Some friends appealed to the Nazi authorities, hoping to save my father, but they refused. But they did allow the rest of the family to be placed on a special 'priority' list, which we hoped would stop us being deported 'east'. We found out later that my father had been taken to prison, tortured and deported to Auschwitz camp, where he was murdered with many other Jews.

After the Nazi invasion, I remember all the restrictions that changed my life and made me different from other children. First of all, I was no longer allowed to go to my nice modern primary school. I was sent to another school and the peculiar thing was that the people sitting next to me in class would be there one day, then disappear the next. They had been sent away by the Nazis 'to the east'. I wasn't allowed to play in the park at the end of the street, or go to the zoo or other places of entertainment. And I had to wear a yellow star to show that I was Jewish – even though my family wasn't religious at all.

In March 1943, we were ordered to report to the railway station to be sent to a camp in the small Dutch town of Barneveld. The camp was in a castle and the people sent there were mostly professional Jews. There were no fences or guards, but nobody tried to escape. We had been promised that we would be allowed to remain in Holland. But in September 1943, the German Army suddenly entered the camp and gave us all 20 minutes to pack. We were being sent to the camp of Westerbork. There was panic and fear – from there we could be sent 'east' – into the unknown.

Westerbork was a totally different place. The railway line went into the centre of the camp and it was surrounded by a moat and barbed-wire fence, with sentry boxes and searchlights. Conditions were harsh and diseases spread like wildfire. Our group was sent to Barrack 85, with men on the left, and women and children on the right. At each end of the barracks, there were washing facilities – a central pipe with taps at intervals along it. There was no hot water. There were tables in front of each window, and between them metal bunk beds two tiers high, and then three tiers high as the ceiling height increased to the centre of the barracks. The bunks were all so close together that you had to climb up at the ends and step over sleeping bodies to get to your bed space. It was terribly overcrowded, but we got used to that. The toilets were in a separate barracks – just a large pit in the sand, with wooden planks on top and holes cut for the toilet seats. There were two rows of about 35 seats – the largest loo I have ever seen!

We had no school, but I played with the other children and we made up an alphabet about life in Westerbork. My mother made me write it down after the war and it ended with "Z is the sun (*Zon*) which will shine once again." We longed for freedom and never gave up hope.

Life in Westerbork revolved around Tuesdays. That was the day the trains would leave for 'the east' – in other words the concentration camps of Auschwitz, Sobibor, Bergen-Belsen and occasionally Theresienstadt – taking anything from 900 to 1,500 people. Tension would start to build up at the weekend. The list of those selected to travel would be posted on the notice board. Those on the list desperately tried to avoid going. The others breathed a sigh of relief.

For us, life continued like this for a whole year – until 4 September 1944. Then the worst happened – we were on the list to be deported to Theresienstadt. I remember this journey very clearly. Mother got us ready – we wore three pairs of pants, three vests, three shirts, two pairs of trousers, two jumpers, a jacket, coat, hat and gloves and carried a small rucksack. We were pushed and shoved into the cattle truck train, about 60 people in all. Then there was a rumble as the guards rolled the door shut and bolted it. It was very dark inside and people were shouting and crying. We spent 36 hours in that train with no food or water and a wooden tub for a lavatory. The terrible smell made it difficult to breathe.

Finally, the train pulled into Theresienstadt and they opened the door. This camp was totally different from Westerbork. It had been a military camp before, but the Nazis had turned it into a place where many professional Jews – university teachers, musicians, lawyers and so on – were sent.

We were housed in a very large stone barracks, four floors high, with a parade ground in the middle. We slept on the floor with our belongings around us. We only got one meal a day and were ravenous. The hunger was always on your mind. Later, we children lived apart from our mother in a children's home. But she would come and see us from time to time, carrying an aluminium saucepan containing a mixture of bread and hot water. She called it *broodpap*, bread porridge. With one spoon, she would feed each of us in turn. I never saw her take a spoonful for herself.

We had no schooling in Theresienstadt. We played cards and chess with odd pieces. We collected razor blades and made torches from worn-out batteries, wires and bulbs. We used to sleep with the batteries between our legs and the warmth of our bodies made them work a bit longer and give us some light.

As the war drew to a close, many prisoners from other camps were brought to Theresienstadt. There was a lot of disease and we were very, very hungry. We heard rumours that the war was nearly over. My mother was known as one of the few English speakers. One day, as she came back from work, some Russian prisoners approached her. They begged her to go to their house because they wanted to show her something. They took her to the attic, where they had hidden a secret radio. She wrote down what she heard. "Yesterday at 2.41 a.m. at Eisenhower's Headquarters..." It was Winston Churchill broadcasting to the world that Germany had been defeated and the war would end at midnight. Mother was probably the first person in the camp to know that the war was over.

But that wasn't quite the end for us. We were still under German occupation. What would happen to us? Then, on 9 May, we were set free by the Russian Army. Not long after, the International Red Cross took over running the camp. We stayed there for another month or so, then it was time to leave. Mother guessed that we would have no family left alive in Holland, so we eventually travelled straight to England. We were home at last.

The Westerbork Alphabet

A are the *Ardapelen* – Potatoes – on which the Jews
have to live

B are the *Baantjes* – Jobs – which we all desire to
have

C is the *Comandant* – Commandant – whose orders
are out

D is the *Dienst* – Military – that we don't care about

E is the *Eten* – Food – that the Jews love to share

F is the *Fijant* – Enemy – from here and over there

G is the *Goelars* – Goulash – which reminds us of
meat

H is the *Heide* – Heath – it's forbidden for our feet

I are the *Ipa* – Rumours – don't need papers for
seeing

J is the *Jood* – Jew – the dangerous being

K is the *Kamp, Kofi, Keuken* – Camp, the Coffee and
Kitchen

L are the *Luizen* – Lice – which give us much
itching

M is the *Macht* – Might – of the military police

N is the *Nethijt* – Neatness – of our WC's

O is the *Ordedienst* – Camp Police – he's so
dangerous and cross

P is the *Prikeldraad* – Barbed Wire – which I hate so
much

Q is the *Qarantene* – the barrack for Quarantine

R is the *Roodvonk* – Scarlet Fever – which brings us
such misery

S is the *Slapen* – Sleeping – on the ground and
bunkbeds,

T is the *Transport* – Transport – oh what a misery

U is the *Uitgang* – Exit – which we're forbidden to
pass

V is the *Vrijheid* – Freedom – we desire so, alas

W is the *Wacht* – Guard – of the military police

X is the *Onder gedoken* – man who is living in hiding

Y is the *Ijzer* – Iron – of beds, rails and train

Z is the *Zon* – Sun – which will shine once again.

Happy, carefree days. Steven and his family on holiday before the outbreak of war.

Bernard, aged four or five, in his back garden in Lingen

BERNARD GRUNBERG

Lone journey to freedom

I was born in 1923 in a small town called Lingen on the river Ems in north-west Germany, approximately 10 miles from the Dutch border. I lived there happily with my family until December 1938 when I was 15 years old. That was when I came to England on the 'children's transport', the *Kindertransport*.

I was studying at a school in Berlin when I was told I would be going on a journey, and so I went home to say goodbye to my family. I wasn't really told why I was being sent away and I set off on the train journey with my mind completely blank as to why I was going. I just thought I was going somewhere else to be educated and it would be a temporary move. It never entered my head that I would never see my family again.

I can even remember what I took with me – we were allowed just one suitcase of a size we could carry. We could also take hand luggage and approximately 10 German Marks – that would be about £6-8 maximum.

I remember I went home from school a couple of days before I was due to leave and my mother was the only person at home. My sister was away at school and my father was in a concentration camp at the time. So my mother must have given permission for me to leave. It must have been a terrible decision for her to make – to send her only son away to a foreign country, with no knowledge of the language, not knowing if she would ever see him again. Later on, of course, I understood that she had made the right decision, but it must have been heart-breaking at the time.

In the end, I was able to say goodbye to both my mother and father. My father was released from the camp the night before I left, and he somehow managed to get on the train and travel with me for about 20 minutes until we reached the border. But that was the last time I saw any of my family.

As for the journey itself, I remember that when the train stopped at the Dutch border, German guards came on board, walked through the compartments and opened some of the suitcases. They took some things out of the cases, and that meant some children were robbed of the very thing that would have reminded them of their home and parents. Luckily, my suitcase wasn't opened and so I kept everything my mother had lovingly put in, including an album of family photos that I treasure.

I can also remember the welcome we got on our first stop in Holland. The platform was absolutely crowded with people and we were given all sorts of drinks and snacks. I have no recollection of crossing the English Channel, but when we arrived in England, everybody went first of all into the reception hall at Harwich. Then we were all sorted out. The younger children were placed with families in England and the older ones, like me, were sent to a holiday camp by the sea at Lowestoft.

I'll never forget that camp at Lowestoft. There were little wooden huts, with no heating at all that I can remember. They used to give us hot water bottles at night. The first night I took my clothes off as usual, but my hot water bottle turned into a lump of ice during the night! It was very uncomfortable. So the following night, I only took off my overcoat and shoes, and it was a bit more comfortable. But I can't remember anybody complaining. Everybody seemed to have great fun. Then, after about a week or ten days, we were sent to another camp near Harwich. This one had brick-built chalets and a large dining hall that we used as a recreation room to play games and relax during the rest of the day. It was much more comfortable and I can't remember ever being cold there.

Later on, when I got a job in farming, I didn't find life in England at all bad. I mostly felt quite happy, except in the evenings when I was on my own. That's when I felt sad at being away from home, not seeing my parents, not knowing what was happening there. Most nights when I was on my own, I would cry like a baby.

The only contact I had with home was some very brief letters. My parents never wrote very much about events in Germany, or how Jewish people and others were being treated. They didn't dare write that sort of thing for fear of the consequences. Anyway, the letters would never have reached me because they were all censored – an official read them and deleted anything they didn't want us to know about. So I couldn't ask any questions about what was happening, but at least I knew they were still alive. Then, after war broke out, these letters stopped and they were replaced by notes of about 25 words sent through the Red Cross. These were even less informative than the letters. But I had a cousin in Amsterdam and my parents used to send longer letters to him, which he sent on to me. So I was lucky to have contact with my family longer than most other people. But even that contact stopped when German troops invaded Holland. From that day on, I had no communication with home at all.

I only found out what had happened to my family after the war, in 1946. I got a letter from the Red

Cross, saying that my parents and sister had all been sent away to Riga in Latvia. At first I thought, "Oh yes, that's alright, we'll meet up again sometime and start to live as a family again." I kept on hoping I would find them again until 1986, when I was invited to go back to my home town in Germany. There I met another survivor from our town, a lady about the same age as my sister, and that's how I found out what had happened to them – and how they had all lost their lives in Riga.

She didn't really want to tell me what had happened to them, probably thinking it would upset me too much. But I literally forced her to tell me what my family had suffered. What she told me had a devastating effect on me. That night, I couldn't sleep at all. It really affected me very, very badly.

It never seemed to affect me when I was at work. I managed to hold all my emotions inside me and outwardly nobody guessed what was going on inside. I didn't want them to know and I didn't want pity either. And so my life in England was as good as it could be in the circumstances. I kept my inner thoughts to myself. But that doesn't mean that I forgot everything. Most nights before I went to sleep, the tears would come automatically when my thoughts went back to what had happened. It's something I'll never forget. And I'll never forget that if I hadn't been able to come to England, I would not have survived.

Early in 1945, I met my wife, Daisy Dunnington, who was in the Land Army during the war. We married in 1947 and lived in Derbyshire, where I worked on a farm for nearly 22 years. Daisy and I had 54 years of happy marriage together, but she passed away in 2001 and now I live on my own.

I will always be grateful to this country and its people for having almost certainly saved my life. I do not look upon Germany as my home country, only as the country of my birth. To me, Germany is just another foreign country. I feel British through and through and am proud of it.

Bernard sitting on the bonnet of his Dad's BMW, aged four

Arek at the Holocaust Centre, Nottinghamshire, 2003

AREK HERSH

An orphan in Auschwitz

My name is Arek Hersh and I was born in a town called Sieradz in Poland on 13 September 1928. It was an army town and we children used to watch the soldiers marching past and walk behind, pretending to be soldiers as well.

My mother looked very Spanish, probably because long ago her ancestors had fled from persecution in Spain. She cooked and did everything for us. My father was a boot-maker by trade; he was kept busy making boots for the army officers. I had three sisters and one brother. We had a very good childhood, playing in the forests and skating on frozen rivers in winter.

Religion was important in our family and we went to the synagogue on Friday nights and Saturdays. I have very clear memories of going to the synagogue at Jewish festival times. It was very enjoyable and I had fun running around with the other boys of my age. I went to a very good Jewish school, where I sang solo in the school choir. My favourite subject was Polish.

As children, we played bat and ball games, and in the winter I enjoyed hurtling down the hill on my sledge in the snow. In the summer, we went swimming in the river. One day I nearly drowned, but at the last minute somebody grabbed my hair and pulled me out. My best friend was my cousin, Rubin, who was the same age as me, but I also had two friends who were not Jewish.

This happy life started to change in 1939, when I was 11 years old. The Germans had already occupied our town and the Jewish school was closed. We had to wear yellow stars to show that we were Jewish and soon all the Jews were forced to move into a small area of the town, called the ghetto.

We also had to go and work for the Germans. At 11 years old, I was taken to a labour camp in a place called Otoschno, to work on a new railway line to Russia. We had to work very long hours with very little food and harsh beatings. But somehow I managed to survive. After 18 months, only 11 people were left out of the 2,500 who had started there – and I was one of them.

When our part of the railway line was finished, the camp commander sent me back home to the ghetto in Sieradz. By then, my father had been taken away and to this day, I don't really know what happened to him.

Two weeks after I returned, in August 1942, all the Jews were ordered to assemble in the market place, and from there we were marched to a church. Then we had to file out of the building one by one, so the Nazis could select people who were fit for work. As I went out, I noticed two high-ranking officers. One of them shouted, "What's your profession?" and I shouted back, "*Schneider*" (tailor). The officer sent me back inside the church with my mother and most of my family. Later on, I went out again to fetch some water and the officer asked me the same question. I repeated that I was a tailor – and this time he told me to join the group of 150 people outside. Being 'selected' like that saved my life. The people in the church – all 4,000 of them, including my family – were taken to a concentration camp and perished there.

The group of 150 people chosen for work were then taken to the ghetto in the town of Lodz. That was a terrible place. There was overcrowding, poor sanitation, diseases and starvation. The people I saw there were thin and undernourished. Once again, we had to work very long hours and every day was a struggle to survive. I felt so alone.

Eventually, I applied to enter an orphanage in Lodz ghetto and was accepted. There I met my first love, a girl called Genia, who made life in the ghetto so much easier to bear. She was a beautiful girl, with big brown eyes and a delightful smile. Everything around us was so drab and dirty, but when I was with Genia, it didn't seem to matter.

Life carried on like this, working hard, until June 1944, when the Germans decided to start emptying the ghetto. In August, orders came through for the orphanage to be closed. We were told we were going to be 'resettled'; we had to collect our belongings together and were then marched to the railway station. We travelled two days and one night, crammed into a cattle wagon train, about 100 people to a wagon, with no food and water and no toilet facilities. At least I was travelling with Genia and could try to look after her. It was the only thing that kept me going.

We finally arrived in Auschwitz concentration camp and the 185 children from the orphanage got off the train. The Nazi officers told us to leave our suitcases and make two queues: men and boys on one side, women and children on the other. All 185 of us were sent to stand with the women and children. There was a sudden commotion and I took my chance while the officers were dealing with it. I walked across to the men's side and another boy followed me. I knew it would be better to stand with those chosen for work. I had escaped again, but all the other children lost their lives that day – including my beautiful Genia.

I had been 'selected' to live – and to carry on working.

My hair was shaved off and a number tattooed on my arm – B7608. Then I got a striped uniform and was sent to the barracks. The conditions were terrible and we had to work hard – with hardly any food. For breakfast, we had a small piece of black bread and some 'coffee' made from burned wheat. Then at lunchtime, we had watery soup with a few vegetables floating in it. I had to work looking after horses and ploughing fields, then later I was sent on a fishing work group.

By January 1945, the Germans were losing the war and the Russian Army was coming closer – which meant that we might soon be liberated. But the Nazis decided to march us all out of Auschwitz on what became known as the 'death march'. It was freezing cold, heavy snow, but we just had to keep walking. It was an awful time. After a few days, we were put into railway wagons and taken to another concentration camp called Buchenwald. I stayed there for another terrible three months.

Then, in April 1945, the Nazis decided to empty that camp as well and we were loaded onto another train. That nightmare journey lasted three and a half weeks. I was still only 15 years old, but I wondered if any of us would survive. Finally, on 4 May 1945, we arrived in Czechoslovakia, where the Russian Army liberated us four days later. Despite all the odds, I had survived.

Three months later, I was brought to England with 300 other children. I had another mountain to climb to rebuild my life, especially after I discovered that none of my family had survived. But I learned English, trained to be an electrician and slowly made a new life. I got married, had three children and now have seven grandchildren. Since the war, I have lived and appreciated every moment of my life.

Arek, far left, with a group of young survivors in Theresienstadt shortly before they came to England, August 1945

You can read Arek's story in full in *A Detail of History* (Quill Press/The Holocaust Centre, 2001).

Outside the church in Sieradz where Arek was selected to join a work group

Zdenka and her mother, who is wearing the yellow star of David, before they were deported. Zdenka received this photo in 1989, 50 years after she last saw her mother.

Zdenka Husserl

I was only a little girl

My name is Zdenka Husserl and I was born in Prague, Czechoslovakia, in 1939, the year the war broke out. I was only a little girl during the war years and I don't remember my mother and father at all. I know that my father was born in Vienna, and many years later, I found out that he was sent to the Lodz ghetto in Poland and died there. I am an only child, but I always longed to have a brother.

After my father died, my mother and I went to live with my grandfather, although I don't remember anything of that period. I know that my father recognised the danger for Jews and told my mother that she must leave Prague.

My mother and I were deported to the concentration camp of Theresienstadt (Terezin in Czech) in November 1942, when I was three years old. My earliest memories as a child date from that period. I remember having my hair shaved because I had lice in my hair – and screaming while they did it. It was a frightening experience for a little girl. And I have a memory of burning my right hand, in an oven, I think. I slept on a top bunk and I remember standing in the snow without any shoes on. One of my strongest memories is of the Alsatian dogs that guarded the camp – to this day I can't stand them and if there's one near me, I have to cross the road!

I wasn't with my mother in the camp because I think she was ill. We were separated and that's probably why I don't remember her. After all, I was in the camp until I was six and a half years old, so I would have remembered her if we had been together. Much later, I found out that my mother and grandfather were sent to Auschwitz concentration camp in 1944.

I had been in Theresienstadt for three and a half years by the time we were finally freed in May 1945, although I don't remember the actual day of liberation. After that, we children were moved out of the camp into four castles near Prague. That sounds quite grand, but the castles were pretty primitive, although a great improvement after the camp. Many years later, I met a lady who showed me photos of children there, but I don't remember it at all. I've been told that some children were quite wild by then and had to learn lots of basic things – like eating properly, using a knife and fork, and so on. I remember vaguely that we used to put bread in our pockets because we didn't have enough to eat. Some children apparently put porridge or semolina on their heads, but I don't think I did that. I was always a fussy little girl, although I was a tomboy.

From the castle in Prague, I was brought to England in August 1945. I have memories of the first part of the journey from Prague to Holland and vaguely remember lots of children running about in the airport. I got very attached to a lady who wanted to adopt me; I thought she was my mother speaking Czech, but of course she wasn't.

We flew from Prague to Holland on a bomber plane. I remember that there weren't any proper seats on the plane; the grown-ups sat on orange boxes and we little children sat on their laps. We landed in Holland and I have a very clear memory of that. The soldiers there carried the little children on their shoulders and gave us hot chocolate and fruit.

After that, we travelled from Holland to England, but I can't I remember anything about that part of the journey. The people who had organized our rescue were waiting for us at the airfield, with lots of committee and press people. Our first real home in England was called Weir Courtney in Lingfield, Surrey, and we were there from August 1945 until 1948. After that, we moved to Lingfield House in Isleworth.

Lingfield House became my home and Alice Goldberger, one of the members of staff, was like a mother to me – she remained a lifelong friend. She was a German refugee, a very good organiser and clever with her hands. I remember she used to organise dressing up games – which I hated, although I still have the photos of me dressed as a sweet little princess. Alice knew how to handle us. I wouldn't say we were wild, but we had problems after the camps; we weren't normal children. For one thing, we were terrified of dogs because of the Alsatians that had guarded the camps. When we heard a dog bark, we used to run into the corners – the Czechs in one corner, the Germans in another and the Hungarians in another.

We were just one big happy family and I think we had as happy a childhood as any normal child. There were 24 children and I also remember lots of animals. I had 24 chickens and we had lots of eggs. There were dogs, cats and rabbits, and if anyone was on holiday, I was the one who fed their animals because I was the most reliable. We used to play games like Ludo and dominoes, but I wasn't very good at that sort of thing. We also had bicycles, marbles, skipping ropes and roller-skates. I still keep in touch with some of the people who were there with me.

I didn't really like school very much, but I was good at craftwork and sewing and I liked gardening. I really wanted to work on a farm, but in those days it wasn't thought of as a girl's job. So I did sewing as a job and worked for top fashion houses for 15 years. I still lived at Lingfield House, where all my friends were. I started my first job in 1956 and stayed at Lingfield House until it closed in 1957. By then we were all grown-up; some children had left the country and gone to America and Israel. It was a strange feeling when Lingfield House closed. The organizers gave Alice a flat as a thank-you gesture and years later, I was very touched when she left that flat to me when she died.

After we arrived in England, Alice started looking into our backgrounds to see if we had any surviving family – and also later to claim a bit of compensation money. I eventually got a copy of my birth certificate about 1960. At first, I didn't want to go back to Czechoslovakia, but since then I've been many times. England has been – and always will be – my home. But my first trip to Prague was in May 1987, the year after Alice died. I wanted to meet the two step-aunts I had found and the person who was helping me trace my family. It was very stressful. I found it hard to cope with people recognising me and saying I was the image of my mother.

On Christmas Eve in 1989, I received a photo showing a young woman and a little girl. I looked at it and thought, "That looks like me as a child!" I turned the photo over and on the back there was my name and age and my mother's name and age – she was 32. It was the last photograph of her. I couldn't cry; I just sat and looked at it. It felt so strange to see my mother after 50 long years. At last I'd found the mother I'd been searching for all those years.

Zdenka's precious wooden heart given to her by Sophie Wutsch, Alice's assistant at Lingfield House. Sophie was dearly loved by all the children and Zdenka treasures this heart that Sophie had engraved for her in Austria.

Zdenka, holding a little chick, aged about 11 in England

Anne, aged two, 1924

ANNE KIND

"We're going to live in England"

My name is Anne Kind and I was born on 16 May 1922 in a suburb of Berlin, Germany. My mother was beautiful and warm-hearted and my father adored her. She was strict with us children and laid down rules, which we accepted. My father was tall and joked a lot. He went away quite a lot in his job, but always brought us presents when he came back. I had a younger sister called Hilde. We used to fight a bit, but always got on quite well.

I have very happy memories of my childhood – playing games, dressing up, playing hopscotch, whipping tops, hoops and sticks and playing with dolls. I liked dressing my favourite doll in her best clothes and taking her for walks in the pram, pretending she was a real baby.

My parents were very liberal Jews, which meant they were not especially strict about religion. We went to the synagogue on holy days and I learnt to read

Hebrew to follow the services. Religion was part of my life, but we didn't celebrate Friday night or eat kosher food. We had a nanny who was a Catholic and my sister and I went to church with her on a number of occasions. When it came to Christmas, we had a tree with all the trimmings, but before that we celebrated Hanukkah, when we lit a candle for each day of the week. I thought of myself as being German first and Jewish second. I didn't really notice that I was different from anybody else.

My best friend, Hille, was three years older than me. She had a marvellous imagination and we played the most wonderful games. She always dressed up as the grand lady and I was either the maid or the nurse. We used to play hotels; she would press the bell and I would go and say, "What would you like, madam?"

I went to school when I was six and really liked my first teacher. The first day at school in Germany was really exciting because you were given an enormous cone full of sweets, chocolates and fruit. It was lovely and every child longed to go to school. I really enjoyed reading, writing and performing. I learnt all sorts of poems and my love of words must have continued because I still love reading and writing. I write poetry now and have it published.

I remember the day that Hitler came to power, 30 January 1933. I just couldn't believe it when some of my friends stopped speaking to me. That day, the headmaster had us all in the hall and told us about Hitler and how he was saving Germany. Then he sent us off to see a film about a boy who was murdered by Jews and Communists. I was deeply upset by it, but strangely didn't connect it with myself. I was only 11.

When my father realised what was happening in Germany, he made up his mind that we had to leave. It happened very suddenly. Father had been to England several times. In December 1933, he told us all, "We're going to live in England." I was full of mixed feelings. On the one hand, I felt very excited – a new life, a new country. On the other hand, it meant saying goodbye to the people I loved.

We didn't have to wait too long because we came to England in February 1934. Hille came to say goodbye wearing her Hitler uniform. But I didn't see it as an ending. I hoped we would meet again. Then I had to say goodbye to my great-aunt Mathilde whom I loved very much. She had been the most exciting person in my life. She read poems and told us stories. She came to England to visit us two years later, but insisted on going back. And we never saw her again.

Our journey from Berlin to London was really awful. It was February and that meant the sea was pretty rough. We stayed in Hamburg overnight and then boarded the *President Roosevelt*, an American liner.

My father had told us there would be wonderful food on the boat – strawberries in February, which was unheard of in those days. But when we actually got on the boat, the sea was so rough that we were very seasick. We were really glad to get off the boat in Southampton!

From there, we travelled by train to London. The seats were so soft and velvety that I thought we were travelling first class! German trains were uncomfortable with their hard wooden seats. The train stopped at various stations on the way to London and I kept looking out, but saw no sign of any place-name. When we got to London, I asked my father, "Why are all the stations called Bovril?" because that was all I could see, no proper place names. Then we made our way to south-east London, where we were staying with a family – Mr and Mrs Shaw – where my father had stayed when he came to England.

I couldn't believe how different England was. For one thing, I didn't understand a word anybody said and that was really hard. I remember at breakfast time, we were given Rice Krispies. I don't like milk so I put two spoonfuls of jam on my Rice Krispies. Mrs Shaw didn't like it and told my mother I was greedy. I have never forgotten that. We stayed there for three or four weeks until our own house was ready.

We went to a little private school and quickly made lots of friends. The teacher couldn't speak German and we couldn't understand anything she said. She gave us an annual to look at and some crayons to colour the pictures. And I said to my sister, "I wonder what this word means that keeps cropping up on the page – T-H-E." But we soon learnt English whilst playing with our new friends. Only two or three months after we arrived, I told my mother one morning, "I've just had a dream in English." I was so proud of that.

I still wrote to my German friend Hille. I told my father, "Hille is the person I miss most. I want her to come over here. If I save up my pocket money, will you help me?" and he agreed. So in 1936, two years after we came here, Hille came to visit us and it was great. When she left, she said, "I'll be writing to you," but then I didn't hear from her.

After the war, I received a letter from Hille and wrote back straight away. Very soon, she came to stay with us. When I asked her why she hadn't written after her visit, she told me that the Gestapo had paid them a visit. They had warned her never to get in touch with me again or she would be sent to a concentration camp. They had taken all my letters and photographs and destroyed them.

When war broke out in 1939, I was training to be a nursery nurse and was evacuated with the nursery from London to Leicestershire, then to Northamptonshire. My father was killed in the blitz in London, which was a terrible shock. Then, while I was doing my nursing training, I met a doctor and we fell in love. We were married in July 1943. We lived with my mother at first and my two children were born in London. I'm very, very lucky. I have two wonderful children, seven grandchildren and five great-grandchildren. And to think I nearly perished in the Holocaust!

Anne and her sister Hilde on the back steps, Berlin, 1928

"We're going to live in England"

Anne playing with Hilde, Berlin, 1925

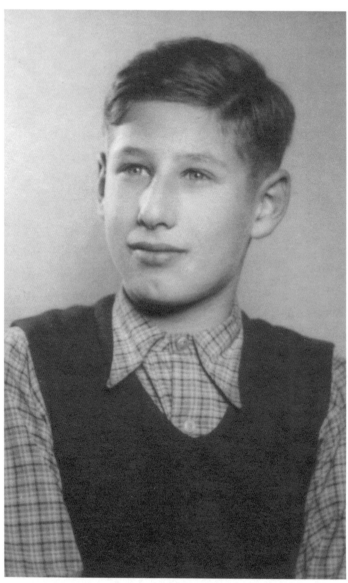

Steven, aged twelve, 1938. Nazi law required Steven to have this photo taken for his identity card.

Steven S. Mendelsson

Hot tea and egg sandwiches

I was born in 1926 in Breslau, Germany (now Wroclaw in Poland), a city about the size of Sheffield. My parents loved music; my father played the violin and my mother the piano. They spent many evenings entertaining their large circle of friends, both Jewish and non-Jewish. My mother also wrote beautiful poems, many of which were published. As a family, we went to the synagogue at festival times. We were proud to be Jewish, but not strictly religious. My brother, Walter, was born in 1930 and the four of us led a happy, comfortable life until spring 1933 when Hitler came to power.

I remember my days at the local junior school, where none of my friends were Jewish. Together we kicked footballs around (occasionally breaking a neighbour's window), and went scrumping for apples and pears. We organised bicycle races round the streets in a game like 'cops and robbers'. I remember that I did a lot of naughty things at school. One day, I sawed one of the legs off the teacher's chair and he fell over backwards! It was hilarious at the time, but of course I got into a lot of trouble.

Round about 1936 – just after the Olympic Games in Berlin – all my friends suddenly started to ignore me. I challenged one of them to explain. He said, "My father said I'm not allowed to play with Jews." It was a bitter blow. My happy social life had been blown to bits. It was worse than being bullied because if someone bullies you, you can fight back. But if they ignore you completely, there's nothing you can do.

Soon after that, all Jewish children were expelled from German state schools. Fortunately, there was a small Jewish school that was extended to take in the new pupils. There was no shortage of Jewish teachers because they had all been dismissed from German schools some time before. Soon I made new friends – all Jewish of course – and all seemed well for the first few weeks. But then serious problems developed at the end of the school day. Crowds of young boys from a nearby German school, all members of Hitler's Youth Movement, would congregate outside our school gates. As we came out, they started to beat us up. There were lots of them – we were outnumbered by about three to one. They had us on the floor, hitting and kicking us.

I often went home with my nose bleeding, scratches on my knees and bruises on my arms.

In 1938, the Nazis made life even more frightening. I remember the night in November that is now called the 'Night of Broken Glass'. Jewish shops were looted and their windows broken. We were warned by neighbours not to go to school, and in the evening the Nazis set the synagogue on fire. Then, during the night, they came to find my father and grandfather. The caretaker of our building risked his life and said they were too late, that father and grandfather had been taken ten minutes earlier. Four days later, when my father thought it was safe to return to work, he left the house in the morning as usual. That night he didn't come back. He had been sent to a concentration camp. We didn't see him for 14 weeks.

Eventually, he was released in January because he had fought in the First World War, but he had been beaten and was in a very bad way. He could hardly stand up and had to stay in bed for many weeks. Walter and I were eight and twelve by then, but we were not allowed to see him. My mother thought it would be too upsetting.

Early in March 1939 – a few weeks after my father's release – a letter arrived offering two places on a children's transport (*Kindertransport*) to England, where we would be safe. England was the only country that was trying to save Jewish children. Then my mother had to make a really difficult decision – whether to let go of her children and perhaps never see them again. She had sleepless nights pondering what to do. In the end, she decided to send us. She knew we would be safe – whatever might happen to her and our father. It was an incredibly courageous thing to do.

The departure soon followed – full of emotion. For Walter and me, it seemed like an exciting adventure, a long journey by train and boat. The rest of the family – who all came to the station to see us off – felt the opposite. I can remember the tears and agony on their faces as they waved goodbye when the train pulled out of the station. My father said, "Remember who you are." The memory is as vivid as if it happened only yesterday.

We were allowed to take just one suitcase, which we had to prove we could carry. It was stuffed full of clothes. Walter and I also wore two sets of underwear each, two shirts, a sweater, a jacket and an overcoat – all items in ever-increasing sizes – because our parents were worried about how we would get new clothes as we grew bigger. We must have looked a sight – huge bodies with small heads!

The train journey took us across Germany and into Holland. I remember that when we arrived at the Dutch border, a German customs official came into our compartment. He chose to look at Walter's case and it was so tightly packed that we couldn't put everything back afterwards. So on top of everything else, we had underwear and socks hanging out of our coat pockets when we arrived in England. We travelled by ferry across the English Channel to Harwich – we'd never seen the sea before – then by train to London. We were in a group of twenty or so children, the youngest aged about six and the oldest, a girl of just fourteen.

In Harwich, we were greeted by a band of ladies who hugged and kissed us. I remember that reception at the station so well. It was a big culture shock. It was a terribly hot day (especially with all those clothes on), and they served us a hot cup of tea when we arrived. In Germany, if you were hot you drank a glass of cold water, but a cup of tea? Then they gave us white bread – which we'd never seen before – and egg sandwiches. It all seemed very odd. The bread got stuck in our throats because we were so thirsty.

But worse was to come. The train from Harwich to Liverpool Street station in London was out of date and very slow. As it came through the East End of London, we saw rows of houses that had lost their roofs or were boarded up. Our hearts sank: it was all so different.

Walter and I were placed in a hostel run by a Jewish charity. There were 60 boys there and my brother was one of the youngest. We were taught to say "please" and "thank you" and with that extensive knowledge of English, we were sent to local schools! But we soon made friends and began to get the hang of the language. We also played a lot of football and a few of us even took a liking to cricket. Today we all drink hot tea when we are thirsty and I just love egg sandwiches!

Our mother's courage was richly rewarded: our parents arrived in England in September 1939, 36 hours before Britain declared war on Germany. We are amongst only five per cent of *Kindertransport* children saved by Britain who were reunited with their families. The vast majority never saw their parents again.

We were the lucky ones, but we had learned a lot from our experiences. That's why I like to talk to schoolchildren today. It's so important for them to understand what it means to be looked down upon and considered a second-class citizen. I tell the children to make friends with everyone at school – it doesn't matter what colour their skin, hair and eyes are. We all have the same right to get on with our lives.

Steven, aged six, playing the part of a lucky chimneysweep in a play performed for his grandparents' golden wedding, 1932

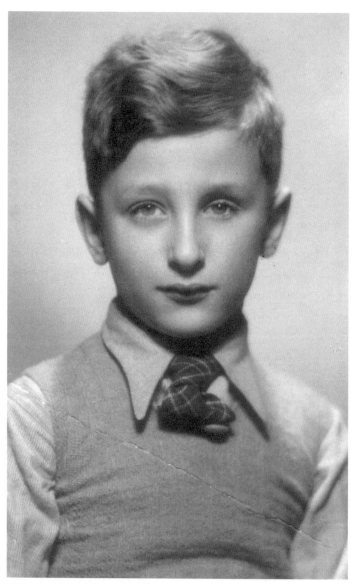

Robert, aged seven, Prague, 1939

Robert Norton

Refugees from the Nazis

I was born in 1932 in a small town called Teplitz Schönau in northern Czechoslovakia. It was a pretty town in the foothills of the mountains, with forests and lakes where we played in summer and skied in winter. My family were prosperous middle-class Jews. We kept the main Jewish holidays, but were not especially religious.

My parents came from quite different backgrounds. Father was from a poor family in Budapest, Hungary, but after the First World War, he and a friend had started a knitwear company. By 1938 it employed about 400 people. My mother's family had lived in Northern Bohemia, Czechoslovakia, for at least 200 years. Her father was a GP, one of the first Jews to be educated as a doctor at university. My mother was well educated and good at languages.

I remember vividly the special family gatherings we had on Jewish holidays. At the most important festival, Yom Kippur, I went to the synagogue with my parents, uncles, aunts and grandparents. The men were in their dinner suits, the ladies in their finery. I was dazzled by the large, circular synagogue with its beautiful crystal chandeliers. To this day, I can still picture it. The whole family would go for dinner at my grandparents' large house at the end of the festival of Yom Kippur, or lunch or dinner at any other festival or time. The table was set with the best white tablecloth, silver cutlery and fine crystal glasses. Children had to be on their best behaviour and after the meal we had to go to the kitchen to thank the cook and maids. But on other occasions, my father would take us to the local pub for lunch. He always ordered a litre of beer to drink – and left a tiny bit at the bottom for me to drink!

As a child, I liked playing football, but my favourite toy was an electric train that my father brought from England. I think he enjoyed it as much as I did! Anyway, I wasn't allowed to play with it on my own!

I started at the local German-speaking school when I was five and a half. I remember my first day, standing with my friends holding a large cornet of sweets. It was the tradition there to be given these sweets on the first day "to sweeten the start of school".

In September 1938, this comfortable life stopped

abruptly when part of Czechoslovakia was handed over to Hitler's Germany. Suddenly, I wasn't allowed to attend school and most of our non-Jewish friends stopped speaking to us – they even crossed the street when they saw us. Jews lost their jobs, property and bank accounts without any compensation. Many people tried to leave.

My father's property, business and flat were confiscated, but his bank accounts were not closed. That was a piece of luck. He had never applied to be a Czech citizen; he had remained Hungarian, so my mother and I were considered Hungarian as well. At that time, Hungary protected its citizens, even the Jews. So while our property was confiscated, we still had our money in the bank.

We fled to Prague and rented a small furnished flat. We tried to restart our lives and Father desperately tried to start his business, but I still wasn't allowed to go to school. Then, on 15 March 1939, Hitler invaded the rest of Czechoslovakia. We watched the Nazi troops march past our apartment into Prague. They immediately started to arrest people. In those first weeks, my father and most other Jews spent every day queuing to try and get permits to travel to other countries. Life became more desperate by the day. Finally, my parents got a visa for America because we had an elderly uncle there. With that permit, we then got a visa to travel to the USA via England – but we had to leave via Hungary.

We left for Hungary with three large suitcases and stayed a week with my grandmother. Then we went by train through Austria and Germany to Holland. At the age of seven, this seemed a huge adventure to me. I remember clearly a Jewish man getting on the train in Düsseldorf. He told my father that he was on his way to Holland to start a new life. Just before the Dutch border, he unpacked his lunch of sandwiches and an apple. He was just peeling his apple when the Nazi border guards appeared. His papers were not in order and he was ordered off the train, leaving behind his knife and apple. As he left, he wished us a pleasant journey – he almost certainly went to his death. We kept his knife for many years as a memento of a brave man.

From Holland, we went by boat to England. During the voyage, my father took me on deck and showed me the sea, which I had never seen before. We arrived at Harwich in July 1939 with our suitcases, very little money and my mother's few words of English. We travelled to London on a funny little train. When we unpacked our cases, our clothes stank because my parents had bought three large salamis in Hungary and stuffed them into the luggage.

We rented a small room with a gas ring and fire in Golders Green, where many German Jewish refugees lived. My parents soon found friends from home who had also escaped. They used to meet every day, trying to arrange travel to the USA and exchanging news from home. Then on 3 September, war was declared. Normal transport to the USA was stopped and most refugees were trapped.

In 1940, we got permission to stay in England during the war. In that year, the German air raids on London started and I was finally allowed to start school. But every school where I started seemed to be bombed a few days later! So I had no education, spoke very little English and had no English friends of my age. Our friends were all refugees. Most nights we slept on Swiss Cottage underground station to avoid the bombs. During the day, I collected bomb fragments from the streets – you could hand them in and got a little money for them.

By the end of 1940, Father decided we would go and live in Leicester, where he had business friends from before the war. We rented a small house in a village called Wigston. I started school, speaking hardly any English. I was a bit of a curiosity! When the other children discovered German was our main language, I was immediately labelled a German spy. Father had to report to the main police station every week, our radio was taken away and our bicycle was also taken away in case we were spies. A few weeks later, a detective brought the radio back. He lived just across the road and said he would pop round once a week. He thought it would be less embarrassing than Father having to report to the police station. So every week, Sergeant Honey came round for a cup of tea and chat, and he remained a friend for many years.

The war finally came to an end in 1945 and we eventually discovered the terrible things that had happened in Europe. We found out that only two of our cousins had survived. We decided as a family that there was nothing to go back to in Czechoslovakia. We had lived in England for five years and become settled, so we decided to stay here rather than move again to America. In 1949, we were all proud to become British citizens.

I finished secondary school and took a course in textiles. I grew up, made many friends and eventually married a local Jewish girl. We have two married sons and three wonderful grandchildren. For many years, I worked as an export manager for clothing companies, then my wife and I started our own business. Like many survivor-refugees, I wanted to contribute to Britain. I wanted to repay the huge debt we owed to the country that had taken us in and saved our lives. Nowadays, I also talk to schoolchildren about my life. I hope that my experiences will help them understand the importance of being tolerant of other people and their differences.

Pretending to read a newspaper, c. 1936, Teplitz Schönau, Czechoslovakia

Henri, aged two, 1942

HENRI OBSTFELD

Hidden in Holland

My name is Henri Obstfeld and I was born in
Amsterdam on 11 April 1940, just one month before
the German invasion of Holland. When the Germans
invaded, I was just a babe in arms. My mother was
born in Amsterdam in 1906 and worked as a secretary
for the Hoover vacuum cleaner company. My father
was born in Krakow, in what was then Austria, but is
now Poland. He had studied to be a shoe designer and
worked in Vienna for about 14 years before the family
moved to Amsterdam. I think my parents met at dancing
lessons in 1932 and were married the following year.
My grandfather, my father and one of his brothers had
set up a slipper factory and by 1939-40 things were
going quite well.

After about a year of the occupation, the Germans
started to make life difficult for Jews. In the first half

of 1942, Jews of about 16 started to receive call-up papers for work camps – and at the ripe old age of two, I received my papers! I was supposed to present myself at a certain time and place in Amsterdam with appropriate food and clothing. It was obviously a mistake, but my parents were very worried. They took me to an aunt and uncle in a different part of town and waited to see what would happen. In the event, nothing happened; nobody came for me and so they took me back home.

That experience must have started my parents wondering what they could do to keep me safe. They searched for a family willing to hide me. I have no idea how they found my foster parents, but somehow or other I was taken to Arnhem, which is just over an hour by train from Amsterdam. There I was handed over to my foster parents, Jakob and Hendrika Klerk, who looked after me for the rest of the war. They were older people, in their early 50s, educated, cultured and quite well-to-do with a large home. I called them aunt and uncle.

My foster mother told me later that there were times when people were suspicious of who I was. She always took me along when she went shopping. After the war, she went to a particular shop and the people said, "During the war you had a little boy with you. Was he Jewish by any chance?" They said they had suspected I was Jewish, but obviously had kept their mouths shut. I also know from my foster mother that my mother came to see me once. She was blond and not obviously Jewish. She apparently came and watched me in the garden from a first-floor window. But I knew nothing about it at the time.

During the war, Arnhem was relatively quiet until about 1944, but by then Allied troops were moving from France into Belgium and the southern Netherlands. In the summer of 1944, people were advised to leave the town centre. We lived near the railway station, so my foster parents and I went to stay with their daughter and son-in-law who lived in a suburb. She had married in 1941 and had a baby in 1943 – the only child I ever played with during that period. So we lived there for a while on the second floor of a block of flats.

I remember one day very clearly. When we were starting to have lunch on Sunday 17 September 1944, the adults got very worked up because through the windows of the flat we could see perfectly silent planes passing in the distance. They were gliders and we saw men parachuting from them. They were Allied soldiers and it was very exciting. Then all hell broke loose. The Germans brought their military equipment from the other side of town and the battle really started. It went on for about three days and there were few buildings left standing. We saw wounded people brought on horse-drawn carts to the big hospital just round the corner from the block of flats.

Somehow or other, my foster parents managed to arrange transport for us all to escape from there a few days later. We travelled in a small car and passed through an area where there was shooting between the Germans and the Allied troops. I remember my foster mother saying from time to time, "Henri, are you still alive?" Fortunately we were not hit.

We made our way to a village called Harskamp, where the headmaster of the primary school somehow knew we were coming. We knocked on his door and my foster parents introduced themselves and "our little nephew". Of course I wasn't a nephew and they didn't tell him that I was Jewish. My foster parents didn't know that there was already a Jewish family – parents and two teenagers – hiding there. They stayed there for all the nine months that we were there.

The winter of 1944 was bitterly cold and the snow lay for a long time. Food was a real problem. I remember that my foster parents and I would go on so-called 'hunger journeys' – which meant that we walked from farm to farm and they asked the farmer, "Do you have a few eggs or potatoes for our little boy?"

One Sunday in April 1945, we went as usual to see friends in the next village. It was very quiet on the road, but when we arrived at their house, we found a

Canadian troop carrier in their drive and Canadian soldiers having lunch. They offered me white bread with butter and jam and I said, "No, thank you" because I had been taught not to accept anything from soldiers. That meant German soldiers, of course, but I didn't know the difference. So the neighbouring village had already been liberated.

When we made our way back home at five o'clock along the farm roads, all hell broke loose again because the Canadians had moved up and were pushing the Germans back. The Germans didn't put up much resistance and fled further north. So we were actually liberated twice in one day! And there was great joy, of course.

In the meantime, my parents had been in hiding in Haarlem – about ten minutes west of Amsterdam by train. They had survived the war and knew where I was. When the battles had finished completely, they made their way back to Amsterdam and found their flat occupied by other people. But my father still had the keys to his factory. Nobody had been there and my parents had left valuable papers and objects hidden in the boiler of the central heating system. They were untouched

One day about three weeks after the liberation, my parents made their way to Harskamp. They had to hitch a lift on a milk tanker and a fire tender because there was no public transport running. That was the day I was reunited with them – after two and a half years. The amazing thing is that I recognised my mother. When I originally went to my foster parents, she had told me they would come and collect me, and I had remembered that. My parents stayed in Harskamp for about a week and then we went back to Amsterdam. We lived in the factory for a while and from then onwards, things very, very gradually got back to normal.

After the war, I saw my rescuers very regularly, several times a year, and I went to celebrate Christmas with them. I used to take presents for the whole family. They had put their own lives in danger to save me – a Jewish child – but we never really talked about why they did it. I still think of them as part of my family. Later on, they were honoured for their bravery.

Playing with a friend in the snow, Harskamp, winter 1944-5. Henri is sitting on the sledge.

Eve, aged three, in Heemstede, Holland

EVE OPPENHEIMER

The last train from Belsen

My name is Eve Oppenheimer and I was born in London in June 1936. My parents were originally from Germany, but they moved to Holland when life started to get difficult for German Jews. My father got a transfer to the Amsterdam branch of the bank which he worked for in Berlin. My mother decided to come to London with her two sons and spend some time with her brother and sister-in-law. That is how I came to be born here. After about three months, we moved back to Holland and lived fairly near the seaside.

My father was rather serious, with dark wavy hair. He liked collecting stamps and train-spotting with my brothers, Paul and Rudi. My mother was fairly tall and slim. She was a fantastic knitter and made most of our winter clothes. My favourite outfit was navy leggings and a navy top which had, in descending rows, ten ducks, nine chickens and eight frogs etc. on it. Paul and Rudi were both born in Berlin, Paul in 1928 and Rudi three years later.

I remember we used to go cycling, and skating in the winter along the canals. I had great fun pushing a chair along to learn how to skate. In the summer, we often went to the beach. Religion wasn't especially important in my upbringing, although I think that we went occasionally to the synagogue. We certainly did not celebrate the Sabbath.

I don't remember the flat in which we lived in Amsterdam. I do, however, remember the lady who lived below us. I called her Auntie Fie. She was a widow who did dressmaking and I used to spend a lot of my time with her. When the Jews were persecuted in Holland, she offered to hide our family, but my father thought it was too dangerous.

By the time I was six, there were lots of restrictions on the lives of Jews in Holland – including having to wear a yellow star to show you were Jewish. I didn't have to wear one because I was born in England – and because I didn't wear a star, I could go to the shops. I often did the shopping for the family, but I nearly always forgot what I was meant to buy! I actually wanted to be like the rest of my family and wear a star. I remember being quite scared on those shopping trips – scared of forgetting what we needed and of the soldiers who were all around. I was always glad to get home again. On those shopping excursions, Paul and Rudi were hiding around the corner, keeping an eye on me.

Everything changed just before my seventh birthday in 1943. We were woken up very early one Sunday morning when German soldiers barged into our flat. We were told to leave. Luckily, my mother had already packed our clothes, food, soap, and so on. She had also made little bags which we hung around our necks, containing a copy of my birth certificate because it showed that I was born in England, and also the address of my aunt and uncle in London. I remember it was a very hot day – and we all wore extra warm clothing as we did not know where we were going. We were taken to the local railway station, herded onto a train and transported to Westerbork camp. I remember wondering where we were.

Westerbork was a very dreary place where we lived in huts, each holding about 800 people. I went with my mother and Rudi. My father and Paul went to another hut. There were other children there, but I don't remember playing at all. We had cards we had to show that allowed us to have a bath at a certain day and time. The whole camp was strictly organised. I don't remember anyone treating me badly, but I must have been very scared.

Everyone got worried on Monday evenings because a list was put up of the people being sent 'east' the next day. We saw the cattle trains and felt sorry for those people. My father's and mother's parents were shipped out to the 'east' soon after arriving in Westerbork. We never saw them again.

We remained in Westerbork for about eight months, from June 1943 to February 1944. But then our names appeared on the list. I think we had been kept there for a long time because I was born in England and the Germans thought we could be used to exchange for prisoners of war. We were put on a train with no food, no water and only a bucket to be used as a loo.

We were taken to Bergen-Belsen concentration camp in the north of Germany. It was the bleakest place you could imagine. There was barbed wire everywhere. Once again, we were in a special section of the camp called the Star Camp. People there could still wear their own clothes with the yellow star on them. I went with my mother to one hut, and my father went with Paul and Rudi to another one. We used to meet up in the evenings.

During the day, the adults had to work – my mother worked in the kitchen and my father sorted out the leather from shoes. Someone tried to organise classes for the children, but it was hard when there were no pencils, books or paper. I spent my time with the other children. It was Rudi who ladled out the watery soup in the evenings. The few bits of vegetable always sank to the bottom of the pot and he used to fish them out for his family and friends. He was invariably caught and punished for this activity.

In January 1945, my mother died in the camp of starvation and exhaustion. Then, two months later, my father also died. Paul, Rudi and I were now orphans. I was only nine years old. It was sheer luck that a family called the Birnbaums did their best to look after me.

Near the end of the war, three trains arrived at Bergen-Belsen. As the British Army was only 20 miles away, the Nazis wanted to keep the 'Exchange Jews' as hostages, and so put them on the trains to be sent to other places. I was with the Birnbaum family. Paul and Rudi were also on the same train, but they didn't realise it at the time. Our train travelled through Germany for a fortnight as the Germans tried to escape from the Allied Army. We were starving and ill. One morning, we woke and the German guards had disappeared. We were free at last.

Paul and Rudi were taken to a town called Leipzig and it was there that they found me. From there, we went back to Holland and I stayed with Auntie Fie for a few months. It was lovely to be back with somebody who knew me and cared for me. In September, my uncle (my father's brother) came to take me to London, but I really did not want to go.

In London, I lived with my aunt and uncle for a while, but found it very difficult to settle down after all that had happened to me. I went to primary school and learnt English pretty quickly. Then I went to a Jewish boarding school. I had visited the school earlier and thought it would be very exciting. I had read some of Enid Blyton's stories and thought school life would be like that. It was a great disappointment when life at school was not like that at all. I had quite a difficult time there because all the girls came from homes that were not affected by the Holocaust. After a while, my aunt and uncle saw how unhappy I was there and took me away.

Then I went to a Jewish children's home called Lingfield House. It was there that my life changed to a very positive experience. The home had 24 children who had all suffered like me in the war. It was run by a very dedicated staff. We were all encouraged to have hobbies. Most of us had pets – a dog, cats, guinea pigs, rabbits and chickens were some of the animals we had.

Lingfield helped to lead me to a normal life. Today, I realise how important it is to be tolerant, to listen to other people's points of view even if you don't always agree. It is by listening and understanding that so many of our problems could be solved – at least I hope so.

You can read more about Eve's story in a book written by her brother Paul Oppenheimer, *From Belsen to Buckingham Palace* (Quill Press/The Holocaust Centre, 1996).

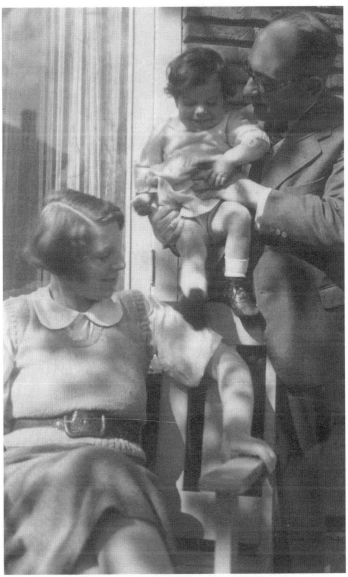

Eve, aged 14 months, with her parents in Heemstede, Holland

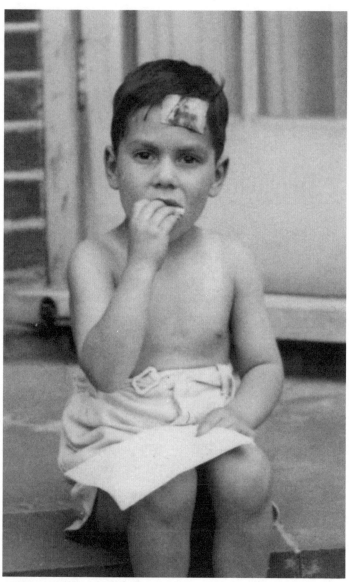

Rudi, aged four, nursing his wounds

RUDI OPPENHEIMER

Surviving against the odds

My name is Rudi Oppenheimer and I was born in Berlin, Germany, on 1 October 1931. My brother, Paul, was three years older than me and my sister, Eve, five years younger. My parents were middle-class Jews, but they hardly ever went to the synagogue. I don't think we ever celebrated Jewish festivals at home. We lived in a nice area of Berlin in a four-bedroomed house with gardens at the front and back.

My Mum and Dad had both studied at university. Dad was quite strict, but I remember he used to take us train-spotting and he loved music. Mum looked after the house and took us on outings to the park or zoo. I have happy memories of my childhood.

I can also remember the German soldiers marching in front of our house with their swastika armbands and big boots. When I was little, I used to march behind them! Of course, I was too young to understand why they were there. Hitler and the Nazis were making life difficult for Jewish people and many Jewish families wanted to leave Germany. My Dad worked in a bank in Berlin and decided to ask for a transfer to the Amsterdam branch. He thought we would be safe from the Nazis there.

By then, my Mum was pregnant with Eve and it was difficult for her to go to a German hospital because Jews were not welcome. So Dad decided to send us all to England, where his brother was already living. So we travelled to England in March 1936, when I was four years old. Paul and I thought we were going on holiday.

We were really happy to be with our aunt and uncle, especially when we discovered that they had an old car. But we had only been in England for three days when Mum told us we were going to start school – which seemed a bit strange if we were on holiday! That was when Mum explained that we wouldn't be going back to Germany because of the Nazis. So I started nursery school and gradually learned to speak English.

By the time Eve was born on 23 June, Dad had obtained his transfer to Amsterdam and we travelled to join him in Holland in September 1936. We lived near the seaside and I used to like cycling to the coast. I was too young to go to school, so I played in the street and picked up Dutch. By the time I went to school, nobody realised I was a German Jew! I loved school, especially arithmetic – and I was good at scoring goals in football.

We were very happy in Holland. But then, in May 1940, the Germans invaded. I can remember being excited to see all the aeroplanes. We children even collected bits of scrap metal from shot-down planes – until we discovered that some of it was live ammunition! Within five days, the excitement was over and the Dutch Army had surrendered. Holland was now under the Germans and they soon started to persecute the Jews.

They brought in laws to restrict our lives. We were not allowed in public places like parks, zoos, restaurants, tennis courts and swimming pools. We had to attend Jewish schools. We had to go and live in Amsterdam. We had to wear the yellow star. We had to hand in our bicycles and radios. We were not allowed on buses or trams.

Things got worse and worse and the Nazis started to 'resettle' the Jews in the 'east'. When I got to school in the mornings, more and more seats were empty as families were sent away. We stayed in Amsterdam a long time, but in the end, our turn came. A German policeman came to our door in June 1943 and gave us about 20 minutes to get ready to leave. We were taken by cattle truck train to a concentration camp called Westerbork.

When we got there, Paul was old enough to go with Dad in the men's barracks, but I had to go with Mum and Eve in the women's quarters. The barracks were big wooden buildings with three-tier bunks inside. You were given a straw mattress, but you had to take everything else with you. There was no privacy whatsoever and the washing facilities were quite dirty. There were even 40-seater loos! But on the whole, conditions were not too bad. You could write letters and people could send parcels. You had to have a shower once a week and there was a school for younger children. There was just about enough food to live on.

Every Monday, there was a lot of tension in the camp because a list of names was read out and we knew those people would be deported 'east' next day. Our family was lucky enough to stay in Westerbork camp for seven months – and that was because of my sister. Because Eve had been born in England and had a British birth certificate, we were not deported. We were called 'Exchange Jews' – people the Nazis wanted to exchange for Germans held by the Allies.

In February 1944, our turn to leave Westerbork finally came. Paul was 15, I was 12 and Eve 7. That day, all the people on the list were Exchange Jews and we were being sent to a concentration camp called Bergen-Belsen. We'd never heard this name before and had no idea what it was like. But as soon as we got there, we saw that it was bigger than Westerbork – and much worse. As well as barbed wire and guard towers, there were double barbed-wire fences and SS soldiers with dogs and machine guns.

We were taken to the part of Bergen-Belsen called the 'Exchange Camp'. This time, I went with Dad and Paul to the men's section, and Eve went with Mum. As Exchange Jews, we had certain privileges. We were allowed to wear our ordinary clothes with the yellow star. We didn't have our hair shaved off and we were allowed to keep our luggage. But like all the other prisoners, we lived in barracks and the adults had to work.

Every morning, we had to line up to be counted. I managed to get a job distributing food and I gave out breakfast – a mug of lukewarm brown liquid – before the men went to work. After that, we children had nothing to do. We drifted around the camp in groups, looking for scraps of food. Every day was the same; it was extremely boring. There might be some watery turnip soup for lunch and four centimetres of black bread in the evening, but that was usually it.

After six months in Belsen, we were starving and looked like skeletons. More and more prisoners were being sent there all the time. Conditions got worse and lots of diseases broke out. Mum fell ill and died in January 1945, and Dad a few weeks later. Now we were orphans.

We knew that the Allies were winning the war and we would soon be liberated. But our ordeal was not yet over... The Germans wanted to keep the Exchange Jews as hostages, so six days before the British Army reached Belsen, we were all marched out and put on three trains. Paul, Eve and I were on the third one, which left Belsen on 10 April 1945.

So began a chaotic train journey that took us all over Germany and lasted two weeks... We travelled 500 miles and were shot at by American planes. Finally, on 23 April, we woke up to discover that the SS guards had disappeared. We were free at last...

Against the odds, Paul, Eve and I had all survived. Later on, I became an engineer and now, in my retirement, I talk to schoolchildren about my experiences. I like to emphasise that if people think something is wrong, they should speak up and not just say, "It's nothing to do with me." Standing by and doing nothing is not enough.

You can read more about Rudi's story in a book written by his brother Paul Oppenheimer, *From Belsen to Buckingham Palace* (Quill Press/The Holocaust Centre, 1996).

Before the war in Heemstede, Holland: Paul, Eve and Rudi with their mother, Rita, 1937

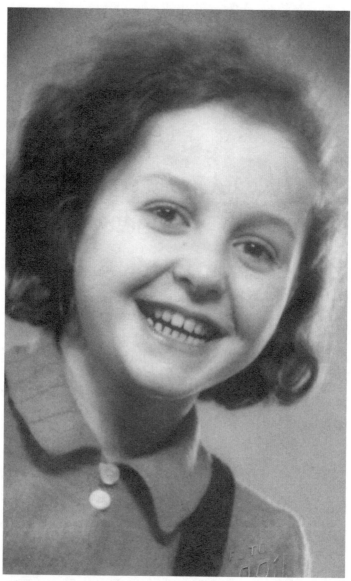

A happy 10-year-old in Prague, 1938

SUSANNE PEARSON

I would never see my parents again

I was born Susanne Ehrmann on 11 April 1928 in a town called Moravska Ostrava, in what was then Czechoslovakia. My father was an engineer and we moved to Prague for his job when I was four. We lived in a flat in the Vinohrady district and I remember having lots of friends. I used to go ice-skating and swimming, do gymnastics, have piano lessons and go to concerts. We went on walking holidays. My life was very full and happy.

My mother had a lot of friends; she loved parties and nice clothes. We were both members of the Red Falcons, a youth movement linked to the Woodcraft Folk in England. My mother was a helper and I have very happy memories of the camps we went to. At the time, we had no idea that being a Red Falcon would help save my life.

In 1938, we moved to a larger flat and sometimes gave shelter to families from Germany and Austria who had fled from Hitler. It made me think what life was like for Jews in those countries. I also began to realize that changes were taking place in our life. My parents listened anxiously to the radio and looked worried at what they heard. They had always had lots of friends coming to our flat, talking and laughing. Now, if anyone came, the curtains were drawn and they talked in quiet, anxious voices. We seemed to be in great danger just because we were Jews. I found this very difficult to understand. Although I knew I was Jewish, we didn't really observe the religion at home. I didn't think I was any different from my friends – and most of them were not Jewish.

I have a vivid memory of the panic we felt when the Nazis occupied part of Czechoslovakia – and then the feeling of total despair on 15 March 1939 when they occupied the rest, including Prague. I shall always remember that day. My parents had listened to the radio nearly all night and were looking more and more worried. In the end I started to cry, wondering what would happen to us. I didn't want to go to school, but father said I had to – our lives must carry on as normal for as long as possible. So I went to school, and as is usual for an 11-year-old, it was my last year in primary school.

At school, the teachers looked anxious. They tried to carry on as usual, but in the afternoon, an order came that all the children had to go and line the route where the Nazi troops were going to arrive. Nobody wanted to go, but the teachers said we had to. It was a cold day and we put on our hats, coats and gloves in silence. We walked to the main road and were told where to stand along the pavements. We were given flags to wave – with the hated Nazi swastika emblem. They were made of paper and lots of children tore them and threw them on the ground. Then the teachers looked even more worried. They were obviously afraid of the soldiers who were arriving in tanks, armoured cars and on horseback. It was a very sad day for our town and country.

My parents and most of our Jewish friends were desperately trying to find ways of leaving the country, but it was impossible because the world had closed its doors to Jewish refugees. Some people were trying to rescue children, particularly a British man called Nicholas Winton. He knew how dangerous it was for Jews in Czechoslovakia and he persuaded the British Government to allow hundreds of children to travel to England on special trains. The demand for places was very high, but I was lucky enough to be accepted – probably because the English Woodcraft Folk had offered 20 homes for Red Falcon members. I can't imagine how my parents must have felt when they found out I'd been accepted. Their decision to send me away was very brave and difficult. They knew they couldn't come with me – and they didn't know if they would ever be able to join me.

My train left Prague on 29 June 1939, taking about 241 children, aged 2-15. I remember my mother packing my case. She packed a lot of raincoats because she had been told that it rained a lot in England! But I can't remember how I felt when my parents took me to the station. Perhaps it seemed like an adventure. I certainly didn't realize I would never see my parents again.

Our journey through Germany was uneventful. The train stopped in Holland and people from the Red Cross brought us cocoa and cake. We got on a boat in Rotterdam – a new experience for most of us – and arrived in Harwich the following morning, where we were given sliced white bread for breakfast. I thought it tasted like blotting paper!

First of all, we were taken to a Woodcraft Folk camp in Epping Forest, where we spent a week getting used to being in England. Then our guardians came to collect us and I travelled to Sheffield. I stayed with the same family for the next five years. They were keen Woodcraft Folk members, so there were lots of camps and hikes and young people to mix with.

Of course, those years were very difficult. I missed my parents terribly and worried about what was happening to them. At first, I received letters nearly every day and they always wrote that they hoped to join me soon. But these letters suddenly came to an end when war was declared. I only received two or three after that. Then I heard nothing. And I didn't find out what had happened to my parents until many years later.

In Sheffield, I started school and apparently learnt English quickly. I went to work in an office, then as a nursemaid in a children's hospital. I liked the work and went on to train as a nurse in London. Then the war ended and I heard from my father's secretary that my parents had been deported from Prague to the Jewish ghetto in Lodz. Father had left a letter and some belongings for me. I knew my parents would contact me if they were still alive. As time went by, I realized that they were probably not coming back. At first, I thought of going to Europe to look for them, but I soon realized how impossible that was. More than 20 years later, I found out that my father had died in Lodz in October 1942. My mother was still alive there in 1943, but after that there are no records and I don't know how either of my parents died.

I married and worked at first as a Nursery Nurse. After the birth of our first two daughters, my husband

and I became foster parents. We fostered young babies and the fifteenth of these eventually became our third daughter. When she started school, I went back to college and did a teacher training course. I then worked for 22 years as an infant teacher, the head of a nursery school and a lecturer in early years education.

Nowadays, I spend quite a lot of time talking to schoolchildren about my experiences, although it's not easy reliving those events. I hope that when young people hear my story, it helps them understand what can happen to ordinary people if they become victims of unfair treatment based on racism and prejudice. I hope they will get the message that today in Britain, we need to enjoy and respect the differences between people rather than feel suspicious of them.

I would never see my parents again

At home in Prague just before I left, summer 1939

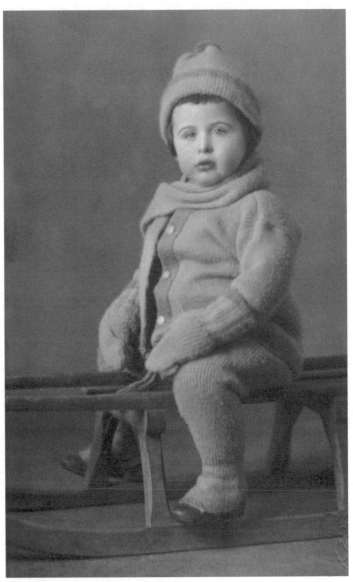

Ellen, aged two, Königsberg, 1924

ELLEN RAWSON

It was all so different from Germany

My name is Ellen Rawson and I was born on 17 January 1922 in Königsberg in East Prussia, a former kingdom of Germany. I grew up in an extremely happy family. My mother was very outgoing, always friendly, smiling and doing things for other people. We weren't rich, but we were quite comfortable. My father was a very tall and thoughtful man. He was a loving father, but we didn't see him very much because of his work. I remember always kissing his hand because he was so tall!

My brother, Gert, was born on 31 December 1922. He was just under a year younger than me, so we were brought up practically as twins. Then, seven years later, we had another baby brother, Heinz. Both my brothers were difficult children and in the end Gert went to boarding school in Berlin and my younger brother to a Jewish boarding school.

I remember lots of big family occasions in hotels, particularly my brother's bar mitzvah, because we were an exceptionally large family. Religion was an important part of our lives. We didn't eat kosher, but my father was head of administration of the synagogue. I used to go to synagogue with him every Saturday morning, mostly because I got ice cream afterwards, I think! When I was little, we lived quite near the synagogue and we went as a family on Friday night.

As children, we played lots of games and my mother used to make time in the afternoons for us to play records – which was quite new then. My parents were great bridge players and I started playing at the age of eight. I also loved and collected books. It broke my heart when they all had to be given away when I emigrated.

I had Jewish girl friends of my own age and we used to meet once a month for hot chocolate. But my best friend was a Catholic girl and we saw each other every day. By the 1930s, we had difficulties because her father was a tax collector and her brother was in the SS, so we had to keep our friendship very quiet.

I went to a very small private school until I was ten years old, then did the high school entrance exam. We had specialist schools in Königsberg for the various subjects – classical languages, modern languages, mathematics and so on. I was fortunate to go to the school for mathematics because that has really been my forte all my life.

When Hitler came to power, life didn't change very much to begin with. My father carried on in the family wholesale and retail cloth business. But as the years went on, things got very much more difficult and I had to leave school when I was fifteen and a half. I remember while I was still at school that Jews were not allowed to go to the cinema or theatre, or take part in anything. I had a horrible experience at school. Our class was asked to give a radio performance and every girl was given a part to read, including me. I studied it, but then I was suddenly told, "No! You can't take part in it, you're Jewish." That really hurt at the time.

When *Kristallnacht*, the 'Night of Broken Glass', happened in 1938, I was away from home in Mannheim, learning sewing. I'll never forget the noise that night in Mannheim – the rabble going down the road, smashing things wherever they found Jewish flats. But my mother had a lot of foresight and had told me, "If anything happens, take some money and take the tram to Heidelberg to my cousin." Her cousin was married to an American and she knew I would be safe there. And that's what I did. I had to stay in the flat all day and night because it wasn't safe for Jews to be out. I stayed there for two or three weeks, but on the first weekend, I went home to Mannheim to get my clothes and personal possessions. Then I saw all the damage that had been done at home. It was horrible.

It was after these terrible events that people began to think seriously about getting the children out, even if the adults couldn't leave themselves. My mother wrote to lots of people abroad and the only positive reply she got was from the Ladies' Committee of the synagogue in Seymour Place, London. They guaranteed places for some children to come to England and fortunately they accepted me because of my father's position in the community. I was 16 then, but 17 by the time I came to England.

My mother told me I would be leaving on a *Kindertransport* or Children's transport, and we started preparations. She packed my clothes and a few small items she thought I might be able to sell in England, because we were only allowed to take a small amount of money. I left in June 1939. The whole family came to see me off at the station in Königsberg and my father travelled with me to Berlin to join the *Kindertransport* train. I remember one of his cousins racing down the platform as the train was starting, just to say goodbye to me. It was a bit tearful, but I didn't take it all that seriously. I thought I would see them all again.

I remember I was seasick on the boat crossing, so I slept all night. Then when we arrived at the station in London, I had a very unhappy experience. There were hundreds of children and people were coming to collect them. The group of children waiting got smaller and smaller, and when it got down to the last eight or ten, I was still there. It was really horrible. Then we were told there was a suspected case of scarlet fever on the train and people were asked whether they wanted to take us or not. Our little group wasn't wanted, so we were taken to Islington hospital and spent over a week there. The scarlet fever turned out to be a false alarm.

Eventually, the Committee lady came and collected me. She had lost her domestic help at home, so I was left to cook, clean and do everything in the house. It was horrible. I just sat on the stairs and cried. I was allowed to eat with the family in the dining room, but I couldn't be paid because I didn't have a work permit. I just got pocket money. It was an unhappy time. The most difficult part was that I couldn't speak English and it took me some time to pick it up. But I did have time off and went to visit some distant cousins.

I was sent from one family to another working like this, usually for just a fortnight. I must have stayed with at least eight or ten different families. Sometimes I was happy with the family, sometimes not. I was hoping to go to a trade school and learn tailoring, but then war broke out and I was evacuated. Eventually, I found a job as a machinist in a Jewish firm and that was my first proper job here.

It was all so very, very different from my home life in Germany. My brother Gert came to England as well on an agricultural working permit. But I never saw my parents and younger brother again.

Ellen, aged four, with her brother Gert, aged three, 1926

Ellen with her two brothers, Gert and Heinz, 1936

Ellen with her family shortly before leaving for England, June 1939: (left to right) Gert, Heinz, Hans, Margarete and Ellen

Bela, aged three, at Bulldogs Bank

BELA ROSENTHAL

Bela's story

My name is Bela Rosenthal and I was three years old when I arrived in England, in August 1945, with a group of children who had been in concentration camps during the war. I came here with nothing – no memories of my parents or family home, no photos and no possessions. It was very scary. Nobody told me where I was or what was going to happen to me. It's taken me many years to piece together what happened to me and my parents, and that is the story I'm going to tell you.

I was born in Berlin, Germany, in 1942, so I was just a baby when the Nazis were in power. Like many other German Jewish families, my mother and father, Else Schallmach and Siegfried Rosenthal, found themselves trapped in Germany in the early 1940s. After 1935, many new laws made life extremely difficult for Jews.

They were not allowed to use public transport or visit places of entertainment, such as cinemas or parks. They could not mix with non-Jews, in business or socially. Jewish children could only go to Jewish schools. My mother was forced to do a very unskilled factory job. My father had to give up his work as a businessman and was made to clean the streets of Berlin.

By June 1943, my mother and I were still living in Berlin – but we were the only ones left at home. First my elderly grandmother had been sent away and murdered in the death camp called Auschwitz. Then my father was also taken and killed in Auschwitz.

Then the Nazis came for us. They broke the locks on our front door, forced their way in and kept us at the Jewish Hospital until they decided where to send us. My mother had to pay to have the lock mended and the apartment cleaned. She also had to sign a document listing all the contents of the apartment. When all that was done, we were forced to go to Theresienstadt.

Theresienstadt was a camp not far from Prague in Czechoslovakia. It had been used as a military camp and had a wall all round it, with barbed wire and watchtowers. The buildings inside were barracks which had been used by soldiers. Nearly 141,000 Jews were sent to Theresienstadt and a quarter of them died there. 15,000 children were sent there and less than 150 survived. I was one of those lucky ones.

When we arrived, my mother went to a women's-only house and I was taken to another house with some other very young children. My mother lived in a room where there were three tiers of bunk beds all round the walls. She had to work very long hours in the camp, but she came to visit me when she could. There was very little food and hardly any washing facilities. The food was just watery soup and a small piece of bread each day. Many Jews died of starvation, overwork and illness. There were many diseases because of the poor living conditions, very little medical care and no medicines. After only a few months there, my mother died of tuberculosis, a serious disease that attacks the lungs.

After she died, I stayed in the camp for a further year with five other young orphans. Women from the camp brought us a little food; one woman in particular, who worked in the vegetable garden, used to hide vegetables under her clothes and bring them for me to eat. She was risking her own life – and she helped save mine. We were kept in a room without toys and we only had each other for company. We had very little care whatsoever. I caught some serious illnesses, but managed to recover. Luckily, I was a strong child – some other children were not so lucky.

The International Red Cross heard rumours about the conditions in Theresienstadt and came to visit.

When the Nazis heard they were coming, they got people to quickly paint the buildings, clean up the streets, print some camp money, build shower facilities and open coffee bars. They even built a cemetery and put up grave stones with names. But there were no bodies in the graves and the names didn't refer to actual people who had died there. They sent away all the Jews who were thin and ill and brought in new Jews who looked healthy. So when the Red Cross came, they didn't find out what had really been happening in the camp. As soon as they left, everything went back to the way it was before.

When the war came to an end, the Russian Army set us free in May 1945. They brought doctors and nurses with them to help look after all the Jews in the camp. I was too ill to be moved until June, but then I joined the other children at Olesovickych Castle just outside Prague. We were all looked after there while people checked to see if we had any relatives or homes to go back to.

In my case, they couldn't find anyone to claim me. That was how I came to England as one of 301 children brought by the British Government to Crosby on Eden in Westmorland. The six of us who had been in Theresienstadt were kept there until October while the Jewish community decided what to do with us. Eventually, they found two German nurses to look after us at a house called Bulldogs Bank in Sussex.

We spent a year there, learning to use a knife and fork, to play with toys, speak English and socialise with others. We had to learn to be children again. We had lots of nightmares and were terrified of dogs and people in uniforms. It was difficult adjusting to a completely different way of life. We weren't allowed to speak German or about the past.

After a year, we joined a group of older children in Lingfield. Once again, we had to adjust to a different place and being with other children. It wasn't always easy because the older children had already made friends and were annoyed when we tried to join in their games.

After a while, the Jewish community decided that we six little ones were still young enough to be adopted. We started to visit families on a trial basis for weekends. We were regularly returned because the families didn't want us. But one day I didn't come back. An older Jewish couple decided to adopt me. They didn't have any children of their own so I became an only child. On the way to London to their apartment, I was told that my name was going to be changed from Bela to Joanna because my name was too German. I was told not to talk about my past. From then on, I was their child and the past was to be forgotten. I felt totally confused.

I started school in London but found school life difficult. I had no background or experience in common with the other children. Germans were not popular just after the war, and I was different from the other children because I was adopted. I was good at all sports, which was the only thing that made my school years bearable.

Later on, after I got married and my three children were teenagers, I told them what had happened to me as a little girl. They understood, but haven't let it interfere with their lives too much. I'm very pleased to see that they are all happy and getting on with their lives. But I think it's very important to tell people what happened to me and my family, to try and stop any repetition of those awful events, and also to remember that in the 20th century over 100 million people were killed because they were different. We should remember that it's really great to be different; we should be proud of being unique. And it's also very important to show that each one of us can make a difference if we want to make our world a better place.

Bela, aged three, soon after her arrival in England

Joan, aged nine, 1949

Joan Salter

It was like going to Mars

My name now is Joan Salter but originally it was Fanny Zimetbaum. I was born in Brussels, Belgium, in February 1940. My parents were Polish Jews who had lived in Paris for many years, but they moved to Brussels in 1939, thinking it would be a safer place to live.

I was only a baby so I have no memories of my parents before the war, but I know my mother was an attractive, gentle person. My father was more dominant. He had built up a clothes business in Paris; he would go to fashion shows, copy the styles and have the clothes made in his family's factory in Poland. I also had an older half-sister from my mother's first marriage. My parents weren't particularly religious.

I can't remember our flat in Brussels – or much about the events of my early life – but my parents told me what happened many years later, and I also did some research myself. When I first heard the story, I thought it was too fantastic to be true! But I was wrong.

When the Nazis occupied Belgium, they began rounding up Jewish men. My father was captured and imprisoned in France, but managed to escape and join us in Brussels.

At first, our life in Brussels continued normally, but my mother was very worried that the authorities would find out about my father. After all, he was an escaped prisoner. So she went to the Belgian police, told them that my father had been deported and asked for permission to travel to Paris. They gave us a travel pass and my mother hid all her jewellery in my nappies! For a while, we lived in Paris with my mother's sisters.

My father also made his way to Paris and stayed with a cousin, but because he was an escaped prisoner, it was dangerous for my mother to have any contact with him. Despite the risk, she used to take us to visit him and her sisters were terribly worried that this would endanger the whole family. It caused a family argument, and as a result, we left to stay in a bed and breakfast run by people from the French Resistance.

After that, we were all taken to a 'safe house'. The Resistance was going to try and smuggle us into the part of France not occupied by the Nazis. In the end, my father was smuggled out, but he thought it was safer for us to stay in Paris because at the time, the

Nazis were not rounding up women and children. So we stayed there for another year. By this time, I was just over two and my sister seven.

One day in June 1942, my mother went to register with the local police. She had to do this every week and there were always two policemen, one nicer than the other. When she got to the police station, there was the usual long queue for the nicer policeman and only one or two people waiting for the other one. My mother joined the shorter queue. Unfortunately, my sister started crying because she wanted to be picked up and then I started as well. The policeman got really angry and called her horrible names. He made her wait outside – all day in the heat. She was so terrified that she waited until everyone had left and there was no queue for the nicer policeman.

When my mother gave her name, the nice policeman looked at his list. She could even see her name on the list, but he just said, "No, you're not on it." She even pointed to her name, but he brushed her hand aside. The nice policeman then sent his colleague to fetch another list from the back room. As soon as he had gone, the policeman said, "Look, they're going to start rounding up women and children tomorrow and your name is on the list. If you've got anywhere to hide, go now."

We went back to our lodging and the Resistance made plans to smuggle us out early next day. A laundry van arrived at five o'clock in the morning. At first, my mother wasn't keen to wake us up that early, but she was eventually persuaded and we were hidden in the van under all the laundry. How on earth she managed to keep us quiet, I really don't know! Then we were smuggled out to the free zone of France (Vichy) and joined our father in a little village not far from Spain.

But we were only safe for a few weeks. After that, the authorities in the free zone, keen to collaborate with the Nazis, started to round up Jewish men. My father was captured again and taken to a camp close to the Swiss border. My mother was allowed to visit: she could stand outside the barbed wire and push food through. But she also managed to pass her remaining jewellery to him so he could bribe the guards. They helped him escape from the camp and he eventually found a guide to take him over the mountains to Barcelona in Spain. When he was safely there, he gave the guide his remaining money to bring the rest of the family over as well.

In Barcelona, the refugee organisation warned my father that it was expected that Spain would fall to the Nazis and that all Jewish male refugees were already being imprisoned. Being Polish, there was a chance he could join the Polish Free Forces – part of the British Army – if he could make his way to Lisbon in Portugal. He waited for us in Barcelona, but when we didn't arrive, he decided we must have been captured. So eventually, he made his way to Lisbon and joined the Polish Free Forces. That was how he came to England in 1943.

Meanwhile, in November 1942, my mother, sister and I had started our escape over the mountains with the guide. It was cold and snowing and the climb took a few days. It was very dangerous and there were Nazi police in the mountains. I must have cried a lot because the guide apparently told my mother to suffocate me with a pillow! Luckily, she managed to calm me down. What a journey that must have been with two little children!

Unfortunately, we were captured at the Spanish border. My sister was put into a convent and my mother and I were put in prison, although the local people were apparently very kind to us and brought us food. One day in prison, we were told that the Americans were finally offering visas for America – but only for children. So that was how my sister and I left Spain, as refugees, in June 1943. I don't remember saying goodbye to my mother. I was only three years old.

So began a whole new life for me in America. My sister and I were separated and I was eventually put with a foster family, where my name was changed to Joan. I was very happy and much loved. The family treated me like their own daughter and I lived a very comfortable life in a lovely home and soon forgot my past.

The years went by and the war finally ended. Then the Red Cross had an enormous task trying to locate people who had been displaced. In 1947, after I had been in America four years, I suddenly found out who I really was. I came home from school one day and my foster father was crying. He told me that I wasn't adopted; my real parents had both survived the war and wanted me back. It was heartbreaking saying goodbye to my foster parents. I was only seven years old and didn't want to leave.

When I came back to England, it was like going to Mars. It was so strange. I remember being met at the airport. All of a sudden, these two people came rushing up and grabbed me and I felt awful because I didn't know them. They were like strangers to me, speaking a strange language, and the first few weeks were horrendous. I had had a very comfortable life in America, but in England we were really poor. We lived in a tiny flat, divided into two rooms and a kitchen. It was cold and there was no central heating. My parents were desperately trying to cope with the past and rebuild their lives. It would take some time for us all to readjust...

I was lucky that my parents lived well into their 80s and I was able to hear all the twists of this story from them. My experiences in early life have taught me that individuals really can make a difference. Just think of all those people who helped my family and showed us kindness...

Joan with her foster mother, Elizabeth Farell, in New York, 1949

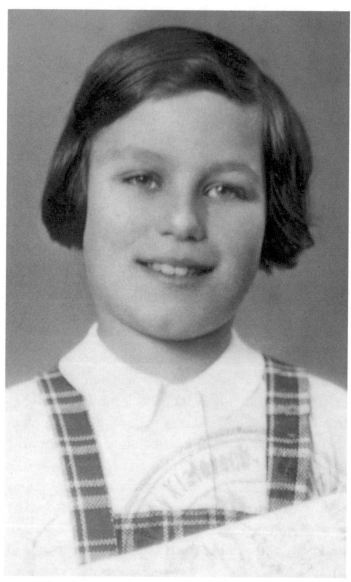

Vera in Klatovy, aged eight, 1938

VERA SCHAUFELD

Saved by the Kindertransport

My name is Vera and I was born in 1930 in Prague, the capital of the Czech Republic. My father was a lawyer and came from Klatovy, a small town in Bohemia, which is now in the Czech Republic. My mother was a doctor and came from Iserlohn in Germany. I love the story of how they met. They were both on a sightseeing tour of Frankfurt in Germany and my father offered my mother his window seat on the bus. They began talking and found they were both Jewish. From that time on, my father kept going back to Germany until she eventually agreed to marry him!

I grew up in Klatovy and remember my happy childhood there. I was an only child and felt loved by parents and relatives, and I have vivid memories of holidays in the mountains and on a boat. I had wonderful toys that I was very fond of – a special circular dolls' house and a lovely rocking horse. I think I was also quite a naughty girl: I apparently taught my grandmother a whole string of swear words in Czech! As a family, we weren't particularly religious – that is, until my grandmother came to live with us! Then we started to keep kosher – that's the special set of Jewish rules about food – and we lit candles on Friday nights.

I had lots of friends. I was one of a few Jewish children who went to the local primary school. I knew we were Jewish, but it wasn't very important in our lives – that is, until 15 March 1939 when the Germans invaded Czechoslovakia. I remember that day very well. Everyone was standing around listening to the radio. People were frightened about what would happen. Then a few days later, my father was arrested and suddenly there was an atmosphere of fear. I was terrified when German soldiers banged on our door and took away our radio, and when we saw soldiers everywhere.

Everything started to change. My mother kept me away from school until father was home again. My friends told me that my teacher made nasty remarks about the Jews while I was away. Suddenly, I felt I was different. Until then, I hadn't really understood what was happening in Germany. I suppose my parents wanted to shelter me, but it was no longer possible.

One day in early May 1939, my mother came to meet me outside school and took me to the little park opposite. We sat down on a bench and she told me that I was going to travel alone to England. She said she wanted me to be very brave and grown-up. She promised that she and my father would join me, or send for me, as soon as they could. They were going to write to me in a secret code. In the meantime, I was going on a special train with other children. I was only nine years old.

The next few days were very busy, saying my goodbyes. I still have the leaving present that my little boyfriend gave me – a little heart with two lovebirds on it. I felt a mixture of excitement and anxiety as we packed. When we arrived at Prague station, my parents were not allowed onto the platform. I don't remember the last words they said to me. I was on the train and could see them waving their white handkerchiefs from behind the barriers. Later, an older boy in the compartment told me that I'd been crying.

When we got to the Czech/German border, my Uncle Rudolf and Aunt Elsa boarded the train and stayed with me till we reached Holland. I never saw either of them again. On the Dutch border, my parents had arranged for some family friends to travel with me as far as the coast, where we were going to catch the ferry to England.

My next memory is of sitting on Liverpool Street station in London. There were announcements in a strange language and children all round me were being collected. I was so afraid that nobody would come for me. At last a lady called Miss Leigh came and took me and two other children in her car. During the journey, I had to keep asking her to stop the car so I could get out and be sick! Luckily, she spoke German.

When we arrived at the village where I was going to stay for a while, the phone rang and my parents were on the other end. I think I cried so much I could hardly talk to them. I was so homesick. All I wanted to do was go home. Even when I had moved to live with my permanent guardians, it was so hard to settle down. Everything was strange: the bread was white, the table manners were different and I could only communicate with signs. My greatest joy was the letters and cards from home that arrived nearly every day, and the days when my parents could phone me.

Then came 3 September and war broke out. Suddenly, all those letters stopped arriving. I felt terribly lonely and unhappy. The family looking after me treated me very well, but I wasn't their daughter. They had only expected to have me for a few months and now they had to look after me while the war was on. I kept thinking it was perhaps my fault. Perhaps if I'd been a better child, I could have stayed at home.

Time passed and I quickly forgot my Czech and German. English became my only language. I went to a boarding school with the family's daughter. All this time, I was just waiting till I could go home. At school, they found out that my mother was German and played a horrible game pretending I was a German spy. It made me feel terrible.

Then, one day in May 1945, a teacher walked into our classroom and said something to our English teacher. She then announced that the war was over. I was so excited I just shouted "Hooray!" because now I would be able to go home. I remember I was sent out of the classroom for making too much noise!

I don't know how I heard the news that no one in my family had survived. It took me a little while to realise I wouldn't be going back home. Gradually, I heard that everybody was dead – my parents, my grandmother, my aunts and uncles. There was nobody to go back to.

After the war, the friends of my parents who had met me in Holland invited me to go and visit them. They gave me some things my mother and father had sent to them for safe-keeping, including their wedding rings. I now wear my mother's ring. I often wonder what they were thinking when they took the rings off their fingers and sent them to Holland for me.

I was lucky to be able to go to college and become independent as a teacher. Then I went to Israel after the war to work on a farm settlement. That's where I met Avram, my husband, who had lived in Poland right through the Nazi period and had somehow managed to survive the terrible events. After some years, we decided to return to England and brought up our two daughters while I worked as a teacher. I taught children from other countries who were learning English for the first time. I knew exactly how they were feeling in a new country with a new language and new friends. My own experiences as a little girl really helped me to help those children who had just arrived in England and were feeling completely lost.

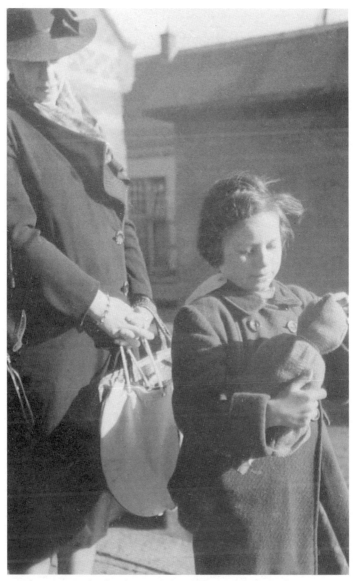

On the way to England with a Dutch friend of my parents, Mine Stapensea,
1 June 1939

Trude on holiday in Crikvenica, Yugoslavia, 1934

TRUDE SILMAN

Shoes on the station platform

My name is Trude Silman and I was born in Bratislava, Czechoslovakia, on 25 April 1929. My father was a journalist, but also worked as an estate agent. He liked football and playing cards. My mother was a slim and elegant lady. She was a good pianist and an excellent cook. I remember her getting up early in the mornings and going to the market to buy fresh food. I was the youngest of the family; my brother, Paul, was seven years older than me and my sister, Charlotte, five years older.

The early years of my life were very normal – a happy family life, living in a flat in Bratislava. We lived on the third floor of a modern apartment block and had a yellow canary as a pet. As a child, I was a keen swimmer and liked skating in the winter. I remember playing cards and 'pick-up sticks' with a boy who lived in one of the top-floor flats.

My father came from a religious background, but my mother was from a Jewish family who just celebrated the main holy days. I remember one funny family occasion – at the festival of Passover. We had a lot of guests for the special meal and my uncle was a bit of a joker. He put one of those rude squeaky cushions on my mother's chair while she was in the kitchen. I remember she sat down on it – and then didn't know where to put herself, she was so embarrassed!

I started school when I was six and loved it. I went to a Jewish school and enjoyed most subjects, especially arithmetic. My best friend at school was a baker's daughter and I loved visiting her because of the lovely smell from the bakery.

In those early years, I was really too young to know what was happening in Europe, but I began to understand by 1938 because we had relatives in Vienna who were already being persecuted. When the Nazis invaded Austria in March 1938, my father was scared that things were getting dangerous, so we went and stayed with my grandmother in the country for a few days. We came back when things quietened down, but did the same thing again in October when the Nazis occupied part of Czechoslovakia. That's when I started to realise that things were going wrong. By then my father was making plans to send his three children to England. Charlotte actually left in December 1938 and went to a Jewish family in London. My brother Paul arrived in England in May 1939 to work for a furrier.

In March 1939, the worst happened and Germany took over Czechoslovakia. I was at school on the day of the invasion. I remember the teacher saying, "Get your coats and go home as quietly as possible." When we looked out of the school window, we could see tanks in the streets. After that, I was definitely frightened, but I was only nine and didn't understand very much. I actually wrote to my sister in London saying, "Please, please, do something to get me to England, I'm so afraid." I only came across that letter four years ago and had completely forgotten writing it.

After that, things happened very quickly and within a fortnight my parents had arranged for me to go to England. My aunt and uncle had already gone to London in 1937 on their way to America. But while they were in London, they were doing their best to get as many family members out as possible. So I left Czechoslovakia on 28 March 1939 with another aunt and cousin.

I didn't have much notice that I was going away. About two days before, my mother packed my suitcase and I suddenly realised I was leaving. I must have liked the belt on my mother's nightdress because she put that in the case for me and I still have it today.

A black taxi came for us, but I can't remember saying goodbye to my parents. I can't remember whether I kissed them or whether I cried. We caught the train to England from Vienna. The journey should have taken 36 hours, but it was horrendous. When we reached the Dutch border, we were sent back into Germany; then we were shunted back and forth, but eventually were allowed into Holland. It took us four days in all and we arrived in London at midnight. My aunt had a duffel bag full of shoes which was thrown out of the luggage compartment and it burst open. That's my first memory of England – shoes on the platform at Liverpool Street station.

We spent four or five days in a boarding house in Hampstead, where we saw mice on our bedside tables! That was quite a novelty for me after the modern flat I'd lived in! Then I travelled to Wallsend-on-Tyne, near Newcastle, where I stayed with a wonderful Christian family, Dr and Mrs Gill, Roger and Joan. It was a terrible shock to the system. I'd never been in a cold, old-fashioned house before. I'd never lived with dogs and, of course, the food was totally different. The biggest problem was that we couldn't communicate because I spoke no English. The family were extremely kind and arranged for me to go to school, but I couldn't settle down because I was so homesick.

My aunt and uncle were still in London, so after six weeks in Wallsend-on-Tyne, I went back there. I attended a little Church of England school and started to learn

English. I was just beginning to settle down when on 1 September 1939 my school was evacuated to Rickmansworth and war was declared on 3 September. Now I was an evacuee as well as a refugee! I remember when we arrived in Rickmansworth, all the pupils were marched up and down the streets. The organisers knocked on doors and asked, "Will you take this one, or that one?" I was one of the last to be taken and I felt as if nobody wanted me.

In the end, I was lucky and lived with a wonderful family. The mother was Swiss and I think the father was Russian. I stayed there for about 15 months although every single night I prayed, "I wish I could see my parents again – soon."

My aunt and uncle eventually left for America, so I was sent to a London boarding school, Kingsley School, which was evacuated to North Cornwall and run by four remarkable women. I really owe a lot to them. There weren't enough people to do the farm labouring so the pupils from the school did a lot of war-work, such as milking cows, planting potatoes and harvesting – as well as doing school lessons. I stayed there for four years, but I wanted to study science and the school had no laboratories. I had to move to another school in Devon, where once a week I attended Bishop Blackall School for Boys in Exeter to do Chemistry and Physics. Then I spent another two years at a school in Reigate, where again I had to go to the boys' grammar school for science lessons. But eventually, I got a place at Leeds University and became a biochemist.

When the war ended in 1945, I had every hope that my family would be reunited, although we hadn't received any letters from my parents since 1942. Eventually, my brother told me that my parents were dead. Father and many of my relatives had died in Auschwitz concentration camp and Mother was among the two million people who were missing.

I married and have two daughters and five grandchildren; and I'm now a widow and retired. I've spent the last 15 years doing voluntary work. I like to feel I'm giving something back to the country which took me in, looked after me as a refugee and gave me the chance of a full and happy life in England, with my family and work.

Trude in her pram with her brother Paul and sister Charlotte, Bratislava, Slovakia, 1929

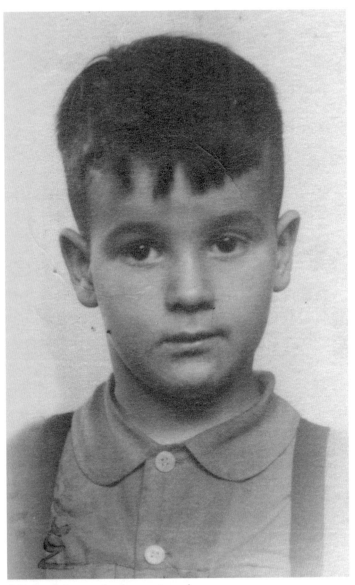

Martin, aged seven, after the war, Amsterdam

MARTIN STERN

I'll never forget my teacher's face

My name is Martin Stern and I was born in a small town called Hilversum in Holland, on 6 September 1938. My father was an architect and a rather serious person. My mother was a very warm person who took me for walks in the park and tried to teach me Dutch songs. They both had great creative ability. My sister, Erika, was born during the war.

As a child, my parents encouraged me to draw. My father also bought me a gramophone that you had to wind up to play records. He was keen for me to take an interest in music and even bought me a little saxophone. But it was really a little toy and I found it intensely frustrating!

Religion didn't really figure in my family's life. My grandparents didn't take it very seriously and my parents would have described themselves as atheists. So although my father was Jewish, I have no early memories of Jewish festivals.

I was only two years old when the Germans invaded Holland, so I don't remember that. But when I was four, I remember being in Amsterdam and seeing the Dutch Nazi Party marching past with a brass band. I can also remember German bombers flying over Amsterdam and hearing German soldiers shoot some men in the street beside our flat.

When I was little, I had great fun playing in the street with the other children. But when I was three, my father had to go into hiding to escape from the Nazis. After that, my mother stopped me playing in the street. Because of the risk, she never told me where my father was hiding. I just knew he had gone away.

The last time I saw my father was the evening when my mother went into labour with my sister. He banged on the kitchen wall to our neighbours – it was obviously a signal they had arranged beforehand. Then my parents' friends, Mr and Mrs Rademakers, took me to their house and my father helped my mother to get to the maternity hospital. I never saw him again.

I was taken to the hospital to see my mother and baby sister, but a few days later, my mother developed a serious infection and died in hospital. I was told that she had died, but I remember it took a long time to sink in. Then my baby sister was looked after by another family who lived about 25-30 miles away. I remember visiting her occasionally; she would be asleep in her cot or in someone's arms.

The Rademakers family treated me exactly as if I were their own son. I remember getting into trouble for trying to pull a fly apart! They were risking their lives for me and did everything they could to protect me. I was even baptised as a Christian in the hope this would shield me from what the Nazis were doing to the Jews.

One day, when I was five, I was at school getting ready with my classmates for some game. Suddenly, two young Dutch men came in and asked, "Is Martin Stern here?" The teacher replied, "No, he hasn't come today." I didn't know that I should keep quiet. I put my hand up and said, "But *I am* here." The two men led me away. I'll never forget my teacher's face as I left; she must have felt very threatened as well.

The young men took me to a school that was being used as an interrogation centre. I was led into a large room, where a man asked me if I was Martin Stern. After that, I was taken to a theatre where the Jews of Amsterdam were being assembled. From there, we went to the Central Station and were put on a passenger train. Our destination was the concentration camp called Westerbork.

Westerbork was surrounded by barbed wire and watchtowers. When we arrived, I was put in a hut for little boys of about my age. Life there was pretty grim. We were hungry most of the time and survived mainly on bad vegetables. People tried to make the best of it and live as normal a life as possible. They put on musical events in the evening and some activities for the children. There was a religious Jew who started teaching about five of us boys the Hebrew alphabet.

But everyone was aware of the train that pulled into the camp every week. I used to stand and watch it being crammed with people. Then the doors were closed and sealed with steel wire. The adults knew that one day they would be loaded onto one of those trains. There were wooden boards on the side of the trains with names like Auschwitz or Sobibor, but nobody knew what these names meant.

One day, I was told I would be on the next train. It turned out to be a passenger train, not cattle trucks, and it was very crowded. Nobody would tell me where we were going. I remember there was a woman sitting opposite me with a baby on her lap, wrapped in a beautiful white shawl. She told me the baby was my sister. As far as I remember, I hadn't seen her in Westerbork as she was kept in a different place.

The train set off, but stopped after a while at a huge German station, where we were herded into a hall on one of the platforms. We could see ordinary Germans going about their business; and they could see us huddled on the floor. After handing in our last possessions, we were forced into cattle trucks...

Now there wasn't room to sit down; we were wedged so tightly that we had to stand. There were two tiny openings to the outside, which let in a bit of light. There was one bucket for people to relieve themselves, but no food – and I don't think there was any water. Our journey lasted several days and nights.

We eventually reached our destination – the concentration camp called Theresienstadt, where I was taken to the so-called 'orphanage'. I was desperately hungry and I remember pleading for food. I was eventually given a tiny bit of porridge – the most memorable meal of my life!

Theresienstadt was a walled town that had been turned into a prison. There were houses, shops and churches, and squares with grass and trees. It was incredibly overcrowded with Jews who, for some reason, the Nazis wanted to keep alive for a while. But people were starving and the terrible overcrowding and filth caused a lot of illness. The Red Cross came to see how the Jews were being treated there, but the Germans had sent most of the prisoners to be killed in other concentration camps and prettied up the town to make it look normal. The Red Cross were fooled.

I was collected from a dormitory for boys by a woman called Mrs de Jong, who took me to her women's dormitory. She wasn't Jewish, but had been sent to Theresienstadt because her husband was. She had never had children, but wanted to look after some children in the camp. She had heard that our father had killed two German soldiers and decided to look after my sister and me.

One morning, Mrs de Jong woke me up and told me that the camp had been freed by the Soviet Army during the night. I was annoyed with her for not waking me up sooner because I would have liked to see the soldiers come in! After the camp was liberated, we eventually made our way back to Holland and my sister and I lived with different Dutch families. I started school in 1945, just after my seventh birthday!

I became a doctor after moving to England and have three children and four granddaughters. I never really talked about my experiences until I was in my 60s. Then I realised that if I didn't tell the story, nobody would know about it. People haven't learned the lessons from the past – and the killing is still going on today. Learning has got to start with young children.

Martin, his sister Erica and the Dutch housekeeper who looked after them (seated), dressed up in traditional Netherlands' costumes to have their photo taken, Volendam, near Amsterdam, about 1952

Lisa in Nottingham, late 1940s

LISA VINCENT

Goodbye to Nuremberg

My name is Lisa Vincent and I was 11 years old when Hitler came to power in Germany in 1933. We lived in a little village just outside Nuremberg, a beautiful village with cherry blossom. I was very happy growing up there. My mother was Jewish but my father was not. He was an architect and I didn't see a lot of him because he was always travelling. My grandparents had a big toy factory.

I loved my time at primary school: we used to write on slates, not paper, and we had special slate pens to write with. I had lots of friends and we used to play marbles. After school, we did all the normal things – riding our bikes, playing in the barns, helping with the shopping. We were part of the village community and didn't lead a particularly Jewish life. We went to the synagogue on the special festivals, but I didn't speak Hebrew and wasn't brought up as a religious Jew.

When I was 11, I went to a very good girls' grammar school in Nuremberg and travelled every day on a little steam train. We had a kind of school uniform – a velvet cap with a gold and blue ribbon on it. There were some other Jewish girls at school as well. In Hitler's early days, I was regarded as half-Jewish because I was from a mixed marriage.

Everything changed in 1935 when special laws were passed that changed our lives completely. If, like me, you were from a mixed marriage and your mother was Jewish, you were automatically considered to be Jewish, whether you kept the religion or not. Jews were not allowed to marry German people. So my father left my mother and took my two brothers to South America.

At school, the first thing that happened was that I wasn't allowed to sit next to my German friends. I had to sit on my own at the back. I felt very lonely in the classroom. Then the other girls said they couldn't speak to me any more at break time. That made a great impression on me and my schoolwork suffered a lot. Then I was told I couldn't go swimming or on trips. The teachers came to school wearing Nazi uniforms and we had to say "Heil Hitler" eight times every day.

Later in 1935, the Mayor sent for my mother and said, "I'm sorry, but this village has got to be free of Jews. You've got to move." We had to move to Nuremberg. All the Jews from smaller villages had to move to the towns. Then signs went up banning Jews from restaurants and swimming pools. You couldn't keep your friends any more. I remember one family shaking hands with my mother, saying, "If we see you in the street, don't mind if we look away because we aren't allowed to say hello to you." I was really sad to leave my village because I was very happy there. But people we knew just shook hands with us and said, "Well, that's the law. You see, you're Jewish and that's the way it is." I didn't feel particularly Jewish because we weren't very religious; I felt more German than Jewish.

In late 1937, a new girl called Ruth Muller came to school. There was nowhere for her to sit in class so she sat down next to me. I was really pleased. We got on well and I thought I had a new friend, although I didn't tell her I was Jewish. She invited me to tea the next day at her house and I was very happy. She gave me the address and I went to the flat. But inside the living room I saw paintings of Hitler and lots of other famous Nazi Party men. I asked Ruth what her father did for a living and she told me he was the new Minister of Works for the area. I thought I'd better tell her I was Jewish and she just told me not to touch anything, to go away as quickly as possible. At school, another desk was found for Ruth and I was at the back on my own again.

I have vivid memories of the night in November 1938 that we now call 'The Night of Broken Glass'. I was really frightened. My mother and I were dragged from our flat and had to stand on the town square in our nightgowns. I remember the curtains twitching in the flats round the square and people standing watching on the pavement. They didn't even say, "Why are they standing there? Those children must be cold." The Nazis were taking the men away and smashing a lot of windows. We had a beautiful grand piano and they just axed it straight in two. There was a smell of burning everywhere.

When I went to school next day, the Head told me that I had to leave for my own safety. "I'm sorry," he said, "but we're not allowed to keep Jewish children any more." He shook hands with me, but asked me to pack all my things and leave straight away.

My mother realized how serious the situation was, but it wasn't easy to leave Germany at that time. England wasn't taking many people in, and for America you might have to wait years and years to get a permit. It was difficult, but Jewish parents wanted to send their children to safety.

Word got around that the Cadbury and Sainsbury families in England were helping Jewish children to leave for Holland. So, at the end of August 1939, three days before the Second World War began, I remember being pushed onto a train in Nuremberg, with loads of crying parents and little children with labels round their necks – huge blue and white labels like you might put round cattle. I was nearly seventeen and was put in charge of some three- and four-year-olds.

We only made it as far as Holland when war broke out. We stayed there several months until we were brought over to England. I remember arriving in London at Liverpool Street station very quietly in the middle of the night. I just remember standing in the dark station and feeling very, very cold.

I found England very difficult at first. I couldn't understand why people laughed here. I wondered what there was to laugh about. I had left my mother behind and didn't know when I would see her again. Fortunately, we were reunited in 1940 when she managed to get to England with the help of the Red Cross. When she arrived, I wouldn't let her out of my sight. I was scared stiff I might lose her again.

But then we were put into a special camp because the British Government thought we might be spies! Later on, I had to do factory work for the war effort. There were lots of things I wasn't allowed to do as a German. If I stayed out too late at a dance, I was called to the police station the next day to explain myself. That was what life was like as a German living in England. It seemed strange that we were given refuge here because we were fleeing the Germans – but then we were closely watched because we were German.

Once the war was over and it was clear that there was nothing to return to in Germany, I got married and tried to make a new life here. It wasn't easy because I still wanted to go back to Germany. I think my mother had given me a deep feeling about being German. I felt that once the Nazis had gone, I would be able go back to my culture and country. But it wasn't as simple as that.

Fifty years later, I was invited to go back to Nuremberg and I even met some of my old schoolfriends again. Since then I've gone back to see them many times. But I'm still not certain if it's really friendship or if they're trying to make up for the past. I feel I'll never know for sure.

Lisa's first class at primary school, 1929-30. She is in the middle of the third row back, standing on the left of Suzy, the girl with blonde plaits.

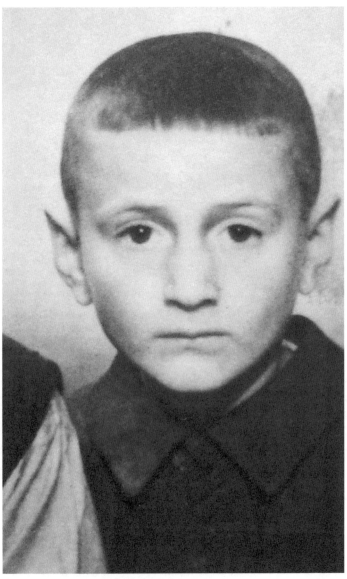

Simon, aged seven, shortly after the war

SIMON WINSTON

Where could we hide?

My name is Simon Winston and I was born in 1938 in the small town of Radzivillov. My home town was in Poland when I was born, but today it's in the Ukraine. Before the war, the Jews in Radzivillov were friendly with the other townspeople – and in fact I'm alive today because of their generosity and help. But in 1939, when Germany invaded Poland, we feared the worst. We knew what the Nazis were doing to Jews in Germany and thought that if they came to our town, they would kill us. So a lot of people fled then.

In the end, the Germans didn't come to Radzivillov until 1941. But they made it clear that they didn't like Jews and the first thing they did was kill 100 prominent Jews. Later on, they ordered all 7,000 Jews to go to the market square and 20 machine-gunners suddenly appeared from nowhere, pointing their guns at us. We thought they were going to kill us. We prayed and cried, and they made us wait like that for two hours. Then a German officer arrived, ordered the gunners to put their weapons down and sent us back home. By then our houses were empty. They had been ransacked and all our valuables taken.

By this time, Jews also had to obey certain laws – we were not allowed to walk on the pavement or own a radio, and we had to wear a badge or armband to show we were Jewish. If we broke these laws, we weren't just fined or sent to prison; we were shot dead. So we realised very quickly how bad our situation was.

To make matters worse, in 1942 the Germans made us move to a very rundown part of town. They had already put barbed wire round it to establish what they called the Jewish ghetto. It was divided into two parts, one for useful, healthy people who could work, and the other for the sick and old and very young orphans. The healthy Jews had to work hard every day, but at least they were given some food. Those in the second part weren't fed at all; they were gradually being starved to death. Then one day, the Germans decided to get rid of all the Jews left in the second part and all 2,500 lost their lives – including my grandparents.

Life in Ghetto 1 continued, but the work was gradually being reduced and some days there was none at all. We knew that other towns nearby were being made 'Jew-free' and that our turn would come soon. So we started to make plans to escape, although it wouldn't be easy. Where could we hide? What about food? In fact, my father had been planning our escape even before the ghetto was built. He had sold all his valuables and converted the money into little blocks of gold, worth about £ 5,000 today. They had been hidden in various parts of our clothes, in false bottoms on our shoes and in brush handles.

Father used one of the gold blocks to buy false identity papers for us, and some of his friends had already agreed to prepare hiding places for us – usually under the pigsty! That was deliberate because it was the last place the Germans would look!

One evening, we managed to escape from the ghetto after my father bribed a Ukrainian guard. We went to the first hiding place about half a mile away, but the woman there said, "Please don't ask us to hide you. The Germans have been and they warned us we'll all be killed if we hide any Jews." So we couldn't stay there, but the woman told us that the town of Brody, about 15 miles away across the river, was the safest place for Jews to hide because the town had already been made 'Jew-free'. So that's where we went. There were Ukrainian soldiers on the bridge, so we had to walk two miles downstream. Then my father waded into the middle of the river, where the water came up to his neck. But he saw it would be safe for him to carry us to the other side.

After crossing the river, we were free – but soaking wet. A woman in a house nearby spotted us and must have realised we were escaped Jews. She took us into her house out of the kindness of her heart, fed us and gave us new clothes. But in the morning she said, "Please don't ask us to keep you any longer. The Germans have been round threatening us." So we went on our way again.

My father went further afield to try and find a more permanent hiding place. We couldn't travel as a family, so he would hide us in a temporary place, then come back and collect us. I was six years old then and I can remember some things clearly. One day, my father hid me in a wheat field and told me to wait there. Suddenly, a group of Ukrainian soldiers found me and said, "What's your name?" I gave them a false Ukrainian name. "Where do you live?" I gave them a false address. "What are you doing?" I said I was playing hide and seek with my friends. Miraculously, they believed me and went away. But most amazing of all, I had spoken to them in a foreign language, using the little Ukrainian phrases my father had taught me specially.

It wasn't much fun in our hiding places because we weren't allowed out in the daytime. We had to stay quiet and not make a noise. To me, it was boring because

I couldn't even play games. Life seemed even worse than in the ghetto. It was very cramped, the toilet facilities were terrible and food was very scarce – just potato peelings and leftovers.

I remember one particular day. It might have been funny, but it wasn't at the time. We were usually allowed out at dusk for some fresh air because the Germans didn't come then. But that day, they did – and we had to rush back underground. The farmer quickly closed the trapdoor over us. We stayed quiet, heard a jeep pull up, then German voices. Suddenly, as we looked up, a stream of liquid poured down over us. Next morning, the farmer opened the trapdoor and said, "Do you know what? The Germans weed on you!" But of course, they didn't know we were hiding underneath.

We hid like this for about two years, then one day the farmer opened the trapdoor and we saw it was daylight and the sun was shining. We wondered what was happening and he said, "You're free. The Germans have lost the war and gone away." At last we could come out of hiding. I was blinded by the sun, but it was marvellous to see it.

Although we were now free, that wasn't the end of our travels. We didn't really have a home to go back to and for the next two years, we wandered from place to place, through Poland and then into Germany. My life as a young boy only really got back to normal when we reached Germany. At last I could go to school, play games and meet friends. I had finally got my childhood back again.

This is one of the little gold blocks Simon's father hid in a brush handle after he converted all their valuables into gold. They paid for the family's escape from the ghetto, their false identity papers and hiding places.

Simon (left) with his brother Joseph (right), best friend Jim (centre) and Jim's mother and grandmother, Nottingham, 1948. Simon used to spend a lot of time at Jim's house.

Where could we hide?

Simon, aged eight, at school in a Displaced Persons' camp in Bytom, Poland, 1946. Simon and his brother Joseph are on the front row: Simon, far right; Joseph third from the left.

The German Home. The first room in The Journey *Exhibition*

THE HOLOCAUST CENTRE, LAXTON, NOTTS

The Journey is the first exhibition to be built in the UK solely to teach the Holocaust to primary-aged children. It tells the story of Leo Stein, a fictional German Jewish boy living in Berlin during Nazi rule. Leo's story unfolds in a series of rooms, which not only detail his experiences, but also those of other children who lived during the Holocaust and survived. Whilst the exhibition reflects a wide range of survivor experiences, it does not show any shocking images.

The 1930s German Home

Leo's story begins in the 1930s German home, where visitors gradually build a picture of the family from the objects in the room. The attention to accurate detail – and the aroma of chicken soup – place you firmly in the Steins' home.

The Schoolroom

The schoolroom offers visitors the opportunity to see 'inside' a typical Nazi classroom. The *Schulbänke* (school benches), teacher's desk, chalkboard and maps are all authentic 1930s furniture. A display case exhibits original items relating to the Hitler Youth and League of German Girls movements.

The German Street

In the German street, there is a smell of bread from a Jewish-owned bakery, which has been vandalised. The clock shop – not owned by Jews – has not been damaged, but the front of the Steins' tailor's shop has also been vandalised. The imposing newspaper stand displays an issue of *Der Stürmer*, the weekly

antisemitic Nazi newspaper. Archive footage of *Kristallnacht*, the Night of Broken Glass, shows the escalation in hostility towards Jews and the damage of Jewish-owned property.

The Tailor's Shop

The tailor's shop belongs to Leo's father and has been tidied up after *Kristallnacht*. Visitors listen to extracts from Leo's diary as his parents consider what to do after the recent violence. They decide to create a secret hiding-place for the family.

The Hiding Space

In the hiding space, visitors get a sense of what it was like to live in a very confined area. Bare bricks, exposed pipes and cramped conditions give an insight into the choice people made to live in uncomfortable accommodation. Survivors recall their experiences of life in hiding.

The Railway Carriage

Visitors are invited to 'board' the train as they follow Leo on his journey to England on the *Kindertransport* train – and to safety in England. Two short films may be selected, which detail both the *Kindertransports* and 'other journeys' – which did not lead to safety.

The Refuge

Set as an English church hall, The Refuge depicts the end of the physical journey for children. The room holds display-cases containing objects donated or loaned for the exhibition. Visitors are invited to discover the stories behind the objects – and the journeys that brought them here.

For more information about visiting *The Journey* exhibition, please contact The Holocaust Centre, 01623 836227, or see the website: www.holocaustcentre.net